D0403031

Godsong

Godsong

A VERSE TRANSLATION OF THE BHAGAVAD-GITA,
WITH COMMENTARY

Amit Majmudar

ALFRED A. KNOPF · NEW YORK · 2018

THIS IS A BORZOI BOOK PUBLISHED BY ALFRED A. KNOPF

Copyright © 2018 by Amit Majmudar
All rights reserved. Published in the United States by Alfred A. Knopf,
a division of Penguin Random House LLC, New York, and distributed
in Canada by Random House of Canada, a division of Penguin Random
House Canada Limited, Toronto.

www.aaknopf.com

Knopf, Borzoi Books, and the colophon are registered trademarks of
Penguin Random House LLC.

Library of Congress Cataloging-in-Publication Data
Names: Majmudar, Amit, translator, commentator.
Title: Godsong : a verse translation of the Bhagavad-Gita, with commentary /
by Amit Majmudar.
Other titles: Bhagavadgâitâa. English.
Description: First edition. | New York : Alfred A. Knopf, 2018. | "This is a Borzoi book"
Identifiers: LCCN 2017025404 (print) | LCCN 2017036363 (ebook) |
ISBN 9781524733476 (hardcover) | ISBN 9781524733483 (ebook)
Subjects: | BISAC: POETRY / Inspirational & Religious. | POETRY / Ancient, Classical &
Medieval. | POETRY / American / General.
Classification: LCC BL1138.62 .E5 2017 (print) | LCC BL1138.62 (ebook) |
DDC 294.5/92404521—dc23
LC record available at https://lccn.loc.gov/2017025404

Jacket design by Janet Hansen

Manufactured in the United States of America

FIRST EDITION

For Ami

My Listener
My Guide

My Goddess
My Song

CONTENTS

Listener's Guides

I

When I was a teenager, I wanted to know the truth. I was always hearing how "all religions say the same thing," but that clearly wasn't the case. In two of the religions, I was going to be reborn after I died, while in the other three, I was going to hell. This divergence filled me not so much with fear as with puzzlement.

After all, the basics in science and medicine enjoy a fair deal of consensus. To this day, I can see the genuine controversy about the best treatment regimen for this disease, or the genuine uncertainty about the etiology of that one. But scientists and laypeople agree wholeheartedly even on the most counterintuitive truths. Our senses tell us the planet is flat and stationary, the sun moves across our sky, and solid things are solid. Our sciences tell us the planet is round and moves around the sun, and solid things are mostly empty space—so many tiny nuclei, each separated from its electrons by a relatively vast emptiness. Our sciences won out rather quickly. Even the Catholic Church's resistance to modern astronomy seemed brief, considering. Eventually they just gave up and went along with it.

When it came to the basics of metaphysics, all I found were quarrels. Why were there so many religions, anyway? Just as bafflingly, why were there religions at all? Atheism, the absence of evidence on its side, had stayed on message since before the days of the Buddha, but atheists accounted for only a sliver of the world's population. I didn't feel a resistance to it—materialism makes pretty good sense, after all—so much as mere disinterest. To this day, I feel for atheism and agnosticism the same unaccountable detachment I feel from poems and paintings that don't move me.

Maybe that was the explanation, I recall thinking. People loved their own religions and diverged in their opinions the same way they loved some kinds of music or art and not others. It was a matter of taste. There was no disputing religion for the same reason there was no disputing taste. I couldn't "learn" religious truth, like a hard science; I could only experience it, like a work of art, or else study it, like the history of art and aesthetics: different cultures, at different times, finding different speculations beautiful. Beauty was "truth," but only in the Keatsian sense, not in the Gaussian sense. Mathematical beauty was universally, absolutely, literally true. Religious beauty was true, too, but only in a private, almost figurative sense.

Unless one false assumption underlay all these contradictions, within and between faiths. Maybe there wasn't one truth to know. Maybe there were *many* absolute truths—as many truths, as many ideas of the divine, as there are human beings.

I simply had to keep seeking until I found my own. I would know it when I found it.

This song of multiplicities, the Bhagavad-Gita, is my truth.

2.

What does it mean to "know" the truth, anyway?

What the Gita taught me—or tried to; it took me years of rereading before this hit me—is that its own assertions aren't as important as the relationships among its characters. The Gita itself has stretches of dry, somewhat complex exegesis. I'm not saying those parts don't matter, but they gain their power through their place in the larger drama.

If you look at religions in practice, the claims they make are almost irrelevant. Whether the dead go to heaven or hell, or get reborn, or go to heaven or hell transiently and *then* get reborn, or get weighed on a scale against a feather, or simply vanish from existence—"knowing" this means less to us than we think.

We go to a religion to meet a God. We don't actually want to know the truth the way we know facts. We want to know the truth the way we know a loved one, personally and intimately. After Arjuna sees the cosmic form of Krishna, notice how he begs Krishna to return to his earlier form.

> *As father would son, or friend would friend,*
> *As lover would lover, please, God, bear with me!*
>
> *God, let me see you again in that [human] form—*

The most common relationship, across religions, is that of Lord and Servant, or King and Subject. Krishna himself, though never a king, is usually painted with a golden crown on his head. Hindus look back to the Rama-Rajya, or Kingdom of Rama, the same way Muslims look back to their religion's early days under the Prophet. Allah's own ninety-nine most beautiful names include Al-Malik, "The King," and Malik-ul-Mulk, "The Owner of Sovereignty." The Bible is full of references to the LORD, to "serving" God, to the King of Kings, and the kingdom of heaven on earth.

Other relationships have always flourished besides this one. The Upanishads, a set of Hindu scriptures that come before the Gita, show us the Guru and Student. The word *Upanishad* itself means "to sit near," as a student might at the feet of a teacher. For most of the Gita, Krishna speaks and Arjuna listens: The Gita is, after all, the world's most famous didactic poem. Eastern religions other than Hinduism tend to favor this teacher-student relationship exclusively: The Buddha and Lao Tzu presented their truths in the form of teachings, not commandments. In the New Testament, too, *disciple* comes from the Latin root word for "to learn."

Our first teachers are our parents. The *-piter* in Jupiter, etymologically, comes from *pater,* "Father." The Father who is part of the Christian Trinity has antecedents as far back as the Sky Father, Dyaus Pita, of ancient Vedic religion. Ishtar and Demeter may be dead, but in Hindu India, the Mother Goddess thrives—and commands, in my ancestral Gujarat, nine nights of dancing every year. She has many names: Durga, Shakti, Gayatri, Amba . . . Astride her tiger, with her sword and mace and crown, She remains history's earliest feminist.

In that relationship, God is the father or mother. The soul is the mother, and the God the child, in the stories of Yashoda and her mischievous changeling Krishna. Orthodox and Catholic Christianity treasure this relationship in the cult of Theotokos, the "God-Bearer," the Virgin Mary. The human "serves" the divine as caregiver. It's an inversion worth pondering: this idea that truth is vulnerable and needs us to protect it.

Motherhood isn't the only relationship religion has conceived for women. Catholic nuns call themselves brides of Christ, and theirs is a sexless marriage—but in classical Hindu poetry, a youthful Krishna and Radha play out the metaphor between physical union and mystical union. The Gita may be austere in this regard, but much of classical Sanskrit religious poetry is not for prudes. Hinduism went on to conceive of unconsummated romance, too, between female soul and male God. The saint-poet Mirabai composed songs that called out to Krishna as her longed-for husband (to the indignation of her worldly spouse). Although this relationship is absent from mainstream Islam, the Sufis used to write poems about the "Beloved," once upon a time; and the Arabic word exactly analogous to "atman," *nafs,* remains feminine in gender.

The would-be bride of a God, across these traditional cultures, was subordinate to her Husband. What all these relationships have in common is a hierarchy. The Lord has more power than you; that's why He is the Lord. The Guru has more knowledge than you; that's why you're sitting at his feet.

The Gita imagined a relationship in which the soul and God are equals. It's a relationship mostly missing from every other scripture: friendship.

3

What made this friendship conceivable? One of the great paradoxes of Hindu religious thought is that it undermines, quite radically, Hindu India's own social structures. India the society had, and has, stark divisions of caste, wealth, tribe, and language. Some developed over time, and some were there at the beginning and worsened over time, but the earliest Hindu thinkers conceived all forms of life to be more than just equal. They conceived of them as identical.

This holds true not just for people but for "the fish of the sea and birds of the air." In Genesis, these are created for Man to name and dominate. In the Upanishads, human beings are merely part of a continuum, forever risking slippage, through rebirth, into nonhuman forms of life. For this reason, the *atman* is similar to but not equivalent to the *soul. Soul* is an English word, and it fits in the Biblical tradition. It was created apart from the divine. The atman is not separate from, or created by, the divine. It *is* divine; it is equal to Brahman because it is identical to Brahman. *Tat tvam asi,* "You are That," is the Sanskrit memory-phrase that encapsulates the idea. (I have since found the truth coded into my own first name: I am It.)

The Gita inherited this idea, and it's this idea that makes the friendship possible. Vishnu enters almost every kind of relationship over the course of his life as the avatar Krishna. He becomes Yashoda's son, Balarama's brother, Radha's lover, Rukmini's husband—and Arjuna's best friend (as well as teacher). After witnessing, in the immensities of Sessions 10 and 11, Krishna's cosmic secret identity, Arjuna cries out for forgiveness:

> *Whenever—rashly, thinking you a friend—I've said,*
> *"Hey, Krishna! Hey, son of Yadu! Hey, friend!"*
> *Carelessly, or even if affectionately,*
> *Not knowing the majesty of you,*
>
> *And if I disrespected you—for the sake of a joke,*
> *Or at play, or in bed, or sitting and dining,*
> *Alone, or before the eyes of others—boundless ever-*
> *Enduring Krishna, I beg your forgiveness for that!*

The Gita enacts for us the slippery nature of being. Krishna becomes Vishnu becomes All, and then, quite effortlessly, runs the transformation in reverse. The whole revealed cosmos reverts to Krishna. Because the Secret really *is* Identity—from the Latin root word *idem,* meaning "same."

Living beings are forever slipping among mortal forms. We call this death. Live through one death, and what was human in this life may well become an animal; live through another, and that animal may well become a human being again. Because the atman is Brahman, the self *is* the other. "You are That" gives immediacy to our relationship with the living things around us. Human beings aren't just part of an ecosystem. We have been, or may become, any of the other species that constitute it.

You can plug this idea, like a trigonometric identity, into that broad-minded old saying of the Roman playwright Terence: "I am divine, nothing divine is alien to me." Every creature, in its atman, is divine, and so no creature, no foreigner, no tribe or caste or sect is alien to us. We really should do unto others as we would have them do unto us. After all, we *are* each other.

4

This is how the Gita balances multiplicity and unity—and transcends them. "Monotheism," "polytheism," and "pantheism" are scholarly simplifications that do not apply here. We don't really have the grammar to express such ideas. The process breaks language. Of Brahman we would have to say things like "It are manyone." Or else, "It selved ourself into myselves." The purer my fidelity, the more corrupt my grammar. Until I recall that Brahman, by definition, is *Neti, neti,* "Not this, not that"—not gendered, not neuter, not self, not other. Yet the temptation to speak of Brahman never goes away. (Not sayable, granted, but at the same time: not *un*sayable . . .)

The thousands of Gods and Goddesses of the Hindu pantheon—and all other religious figures—are seen as diffractions of Brahman into imagination and history. *Syncretism* is the wrong word. Hinduism does not syncretize, it devours and incorporates. That is why the Buddha, after a long period of rivalry, got absorbed into the sequence of Vishnu's avatars, and why Mahatma Gandhi used to quote Jesus at every prayer meeting but had no interest in converting to Christianity. The scripture central to Gandhi's life was the Gita—he translated it, prepared a commentary on it, and recited or heard it daily—and the Gita teaches your center to hold by delighting in diversity, in multiplicity.

> *Devotees of Gods go to the Gods;*
> *Devotees of forefathers go to forefathers;*
> *Devotees of spirits go to spirits.*

The Gita is a scripture which, in spite of its military setting, stays clear of the lust for universal domination. This verse, for example, shows the Gita embracing and authorizing forms of worship thought of as "primitive" or "outmoded." Theism, even then the most common form of worship, shares space with ancestor worship and animism. Ancestor worship venerates a tradition and gains wisdom and strength from the dead, or a partly imaginary idea of the dead. (Today you can see it in the American veneration of the Founding Fathers—that is, of the white male landowning oligarchs who serve, today, as the inspiration for a purer, more inclusive democracy.) I picked the word *spirits* to translate *bhutani,* a Sanskrit word that could be Englished equally as *beings* and as *creatures.* This choice connected *bhutani* with the Latin *anima,* which became, etymologically, the root word of *animism.* According to Vedantic thought, the living atman is divine, in trees and animals as in Gods and Goddesses. The animist lighting incense before a local tree, therefore, does something metaphysically valid. Modern-day environmentalism is an attempt to return to the mindset that once held trees and rivers sacred. It justifies itself with reasons but gains its fervor from this instinctive faith, suppressed for generations.

This is not the Gita's only multiplicity. The three yogas of knowledge, action, and devotion offer more than one way of "yoking," or (re)joining, the human to the divine. Our behaviors are not the results of the angel and the devil sitting on either shoulder. The three gunas, Purity, Power, and Darkness, braid themselves into a personality, and each guna branches out, in Krishna's description, into a dozen or so characteristics. This embrace of multiplicity reflects itself structurally in the variety of tones and strategies Krishna uses with Arjuna—strict and berating, detached and philosophical, tender and personable.

So the Gita's universe is profuse without confusion. What about someone who wants to follow the Gita in his or her life? Embracing all these multiplicities, acknowledging so many perspectives as valid, what do you exclude and resist? If you are so many ways at once, who are you, really?

All these questions can be collapsed into one immediate and very specific question. Luckily for us, it's the same question this God's song was meant to answer in the first place.

What do you do when the other fellow wants to kill you?

5

This requires a word or two about the Gita and history. Not the Gita's own history, which is very uncertain and quite possibly irrelevant. Did Krishna "really" sing it? Did Vyasa, the poet of the *Mahabharata,* transcribe it? Does Vyasa even exist, or is he, like Homer, a construct? Was the Gita written centuries later by that omnipresent genius, Anonymous? Was it inserted into the *Mahabharata,* which is known to have proliferated episodes like a modern fan-fiction website?

None of this matters to our experience of the Gita. Such questions matter more to historians, who regard the Gita not as a life-guide but as a "text," and to people who want to discredit the Gita by proving its fallible human origin—never quite getting that the human can *be* divine, in the Gita's worldview. So I am going to bypass the Gita's history and "mythistory" alike.

I want to explain instead the Gita's place in Hindu history. A millennium of free speculation and religious multiplicity in India had allowed hundreds of sects, cults, and schools of philosophy to flourish. Even atheism had its sages; the Samkhya school, which Krishna mentions so reverently, was an atheistic one. In India, religion flourished on the principle of the rainforest.

The Gita, no matter its exact date of composition or transcription, clearly arrives on a scene crowded with philosophers. At one point, Krishna recounts a statement of materialism or nihilism. It sounds contemporary, but such ideas were tired even then.

"No truth, no base," they say, "no lord
Is in the world. It came to be,
But one thing doesn't follow from another.
What else causes it but lust?"

Holding to this view,
Lost souls with small minds
Emerge as enemies, cruel
In action, to destroy the world.

Do rituals today seem shucked of their meaning—stiff, rote, empty? Does the priesthood seem corrupt? Krishna seems as irked with hypocritical Brahmins as any campus atheist with the Catholic Church.

Such flowery words they declaim, these
Ignoramuses! Delighting,
Partha, in the letter of the Veda,
Saying there is nothing else. . . .

They act out many different rituals
With the goal of glut and grandeur.

Krishna's song of multiplicities is always aware of other schools and outlooks. When discussing union through knowledge (*gyana-yoga*), he seems partial to the Samkhya school of thought, one of the oldest. But his panoptic view of Indian religious thought sees into the future, too. His discussion of devotional worship would resonate with vernacular Bhakti poets more than a thousand years later. The Gita's discussion of *karma-yoga,* the yoga of Action, would inform, through Mahatma Gandhi, the Indian Independence struggle. Its central idea—focus on the action itself, not the result of it—sustained Indians through year after futile year of jail time and failed negotiations.

For all that acceptance of multiplicity, though, Krishna has favorites. Extended passages in the Gita provide detailed portraits of the ideal seeker. Krishna even describes the way such a seeker prepares his seat before meditating. Krishna acknowledges the difficulty of meeting that ideal, of course, and even tiers the different ways of reaching him.

Keep your mind on me alone,
Have me absorb your intellect,
And from then on, without a doubt,
You will reside in me.

Or, if you just can't keep on
Thinking steadily of me,
Then practice yoga, Arjuna,
To seek and reach me.

If you cannot even practice that,
Make my works your highest goal.
Merely doing work for me,
You will reach perfection.

If even this *is something that you can't*
Quite do, take refuge in my power.

Let go of all the fruits of action
And act with self-control.

Devotion is the one thing that must not be lost. Devotion, as it turns out, is the one emotion underlying all relationships between a human subject (or lover or parent or child or student) and his or her divine object.

Krishna motivates Arjuna by conjuring, in more than one chapter, an ideal human being, an aspirant to aspire toward. This portrait is familiar from the Upanishads, seated and meditative and full of serenely wise qualities.

Holding torso, head, and neck upright,
Motionless, steady,
Staring at the tip of his own nose,
Not looking in any direction.

To connect this detached ideal to the ethos of the righteous warrior, the resister of evil, to assert that you can *be* that meditating aspirant and *still* fight hard in the arena of history: This is Krishna's masterstroke. It had no precedent, to my knowledge, in all of Hindu thought.

It came just in time.

6

Classical India's rainforest-profuse spirituality expressed its strength and life. That profusion, had it not been for the Gita, might have been a fatal weakness.

The past two millennia have seen a drastic, worldwide loss of theodiversity. Today we are living through an age of rapid biological extinctions; in the age preceding the Anthropocene, people exterminated deities instead of beetles.

Tellingly, the original Pantheon was a shrine "to all the Gods" built by Agrippa, twenty-five years before Christ. Today it is the Church of Santa Maria Rotonda. A much earlier pantheon could be found in Arabia, a shrine full of statues and sacred objects set side by side: the Ka'aba. Polytheistic traditions of the Near East, Europe, Africa, the Americas, and Australia were crowded out by one of two invasive species of monotheism. After two millennia of extinctions worldwide, only the Hindu pantheon—*pan + theion,* "All Holy"—would survive.

And not for want of exposure to the pesticides and chain saws. Hindu India had already spawned its proselytizing heresy. Just as Jesus was born a Jew, Gautama Buddha was born a Hindu. Some centuries later, the Mauryan emperors adopted the new religion just as Constantine adopted Christianity. After that, Hindu India lived for nearly a thousand years under Muslim warlords and emperors. Some, like Akbar, picked up the pluralism in their environment, while others, like Ibrahim Lodi and Aurangzeb, slaughtered infidels in the grand old style. In the best cases, these rulers were effete rose sniffers and sherbet sippers, taxing their peasants to build lavish mausoleums for dead begums. In the worst cases, they were Taliban warlords before their time.

After Muslim rule, India came under European domination for two centuries. Great Britain's religious proselytizing *increased* over time, as laissez-faire East India Company hands gave way to hymn-singing Victorian sahibs and memsahibs.

How did Hindu India—with no native horses, a technological disadvantage in weaponry, and little political or social unity—survive?

There are physical reasons, of course. The subcontinent had enough disease already, so smallpox couldn't wipe its inhabitants out, as it did the "Indians" on the other side of the world. The Hindus had numbers on their side. Slaughter on the necessary, industrial scale simply was not possible until the twentieth century. Hinduism also had an orthodox priestly class, insufferably convinced of its own superiority. This supremacism, however odious to outsiders, is a sine qua non when it comes to building an empire—or resisting one. The Jews have it in their rabbis; the Hindus have it in their Brahmins. Both are survivor religions, and both, accordingly, are hated. Simply by living on, they cast into doubt the universalist fantasies of the faiths that have failed to destroy them.

Of course, these factors aren't enough to guarantee the survival of a tradition. Physical factors help ensure the physical survival of the people. Hinduism's *spiritual* survival owes much to the Gita. The hymns of the Vedas, the high philosophy of the Upanishads, the fantastic tales of the Puranas each had their place and appeal. Yet each one had equivalents in the bygone pagan civilizations of the classical Mediterranean world or Persia.

Only the Hindus had *armor,* and that armor was the Gita. As late as 1919 C.E., Mahatma Gandhi could use it to stiffen the resolve of his followers against the British Raj. You hold the scripture he sang before dawn on the day of his assassination.

Indestructibility: Be aware
It spreads through all this.
Destroying this imperishable part
Is something no one can accomplish.

They say these bodies that embody
Indestructible, immeasurable
Eternities must have an end.
So fight, Arjuna!

7

I have been rereading the Gita for a quarter of a century. Now, after a crash self-study of Sanskrit and word-by-word research that didn't feel as tedious as it would have been with any other book, I have translated it. I can't really explain how I ended up here.

I was born in the United States into a secularized Hindu family. We are all four of us medical doctors, and no one else in my family is particularly religious. My parents maintain a small shrine in the corner of the master bedroom. Whenever we were on a plane, my mother would produce from her purse, before takeoff, a small laminated card with images of Ganesha and Durga. I had to touch my right ring finger to it and then to my forehead so the plane wouldn't crash. As for scriptures, I sought them out by myself. I found my Gods in the library.

There weren't any books of fiction or poetry in the house, either, only medical journals and textbooks. They held, and hold to this day, though I, too, am a doctor, no interest for me. So I found all humankind in the library as well.

I have never gone hungry. I have never gone thirsty. When I was a boy, I wanted objects but didn't get them; I must have internalized those restraints, because now I do not want objects. I have never not gotten something I needed, and my loving, hardworking immigrant parents saw to that. I do not know why religiosity has surged in me. It is an incongruity I hide from the other bespectacled Indian doctors of my cohort, entering middle age like me, trying to stay fit like me, suburban and midwestern like me. My wife is the only person I can talk to about these things; and someday, when they are older, I trust, my children.

Yet I am least religious in a congregation. I dislike a crowd of the like-minded. I have come to realize that religion and literature are things I learned to treasure when I was alone in early adolescence. Dead writers and living Gods became my truest friends, and I prefer to be alone with them.

The Gita must have played into this. It is the greatest poem of *friendship,* after all, in any language. Twenty-five years ago, a friendless, nearsighted brown kid set it at the center of his universe. It has been there ever since.

Amit Majmudar
DUBLIN, OHIO
OCTOBER 2016

A NOTE ON THE WORDS
I DIDN'T TRANSLATE

This translation contains a few words that are transliterated directly from Sanskrit into English. They express concepts absent from the Western tradition, and hence from English itself.

GUNA

Animals and insects are entirely what they are. Their inner lives (judged from the outside, at least) possess a oneness that is alien to human beings. I guess it's this that led more than one tradition to deny them souls. We experience internal conflicts in a way they don't, or don't seem to.

Intensely dualistic traditions, like the major monotheistic ones, set an angel and a devil on your shoulders. Freud imagines your selfhood in three parts: id, ego, and superego; premodern European medicine imagined four humors: yellow bile, black bile, blood, and phlegm; modern Western medicine tallies more than a hundred neurotransmitters (and counting).

Session 16 describes our natures as either "divine" or "demonic," in the dualist fashion; toward the end of Session 18, people are divided into four groupings, corresponding to the four traditional castes, each with its own dharma.

Elsewhere, and much more extensively, the Gita describes three factors in a braid, and these are the gunas. I won't go into each guna here because the Gita does so at length. That is the same reason I didn't translate the word. *Attribute* and *trait* are not the right words because the gunas are best thought of as *groups* of traits. The specific traits that come under each heading are numerous; the Gita spends several verses listing telltale traits of each guna, or describing what faith or resolve or charity looks like under the influence of this or that guna. So the hundredfold nature of the human being, too, finds its way into the Gita's outlook. The Gita, in keeping with the spirit of multiplicity, manages to have it every way at once.

DHARMA

Sometimes the word *dharma* gets translated as *duty,* sometimes as *law.* Depending on the context, English translators also use *righteousness.* The word seems to hang, ungraspably cloudlike, over a few related concepts. I would like to condense its meanings into prose for a moment, then turn it back into the mist of the original Sanskrit.

Everybody has his or her dharma, as an individual. More than one dharma, in fact: You have certain obligations as a son or daughter, wife or husband, mother or father, and so on; certain obligations, too, as a member of society. In this sense, dharma relates to the various roles we have in life. There is no handbook that details exactly, in a ten-point to-do (or not-to-do) list, what your dharma is. Some ancient treatises, like the *Law-Book of Manu,* have tried to do this, but they have always fallen away, while the concept of dharma hasn't.

This *indefinite* aspect is, to my mind, crucial. It makes *law* the wrong English word. Each person has his or her own dharma. Deciding the proper dharmic action is not always easy. (Note how *proper* comes from the Latin *proprius,* "one's own.") Arjuna's despair arises from the conflict between his dharma as a family member and his dharma as a warrior.

Notice that Krishna solves Arjuna's dharma dilemma by signaling toward the larger sense of dharma. This is dharma in its collective sense, at the level of society, of humankind itself. Krishna promises to reestablish it by taking a mortal birth, time and time again, whenever he is needed.

The Gita is occasioned by a moment of supreme tension between these two simultaneous definitions of dharma. An action which may seem personally adharmic (shooting your own cousins, in Arjuna's case) can uphold the larger dharma.

Fanatics and madmen, such as exist in every society and twist every scripture, have never seized on this idea to justify slaughter. In India, that is: Heinrich Himmler kept a copy of the Gita in his pocket, and he was recorded as calling it the ideal scripture to shape the SS man for his "most difficult task." Himmler's October 1943 Posen speech is the negative image of the Gita, the Gita's ethics of compassionate contemplative action as reinterpreted by the thieving, usurping, power-seeking, murderous Kauravas: "We have the moral right, we had the duty to our people to do it, to kill this people who would kill us. . . . And we have suffered no defect within us, in our soul, or in our character."

The word *dharma* has already entered English. Google's Ngram viewer, which tracks the frequency of use of specific words, shows its sudden upsweep in the 1960s. Rather than switch among three or four approximate words, I have kept this word intact.

No English word could convey its etymological beauty. *Dharma* has its origin in the Sanskrit root *dhrt,* meaning "basis" or "support." It is related to the word for "earth," *dharti*. Societies are built on dharma just as cities are built on the earth. One supports the other; if one gets corrupted, the other sinks. As early as Session 1, Arjuna envisions how the corruption of dharma makes a civilization sink—first morally, and then out of history entirely.

To this end, I should point out that Hindus, when the Gita was written, never called themselves Hindus or their religion Hinduism. They spoke of it—if they thought of it at all in such a detached and self-reflexive way—as *sanatan dharma,* the eternal dharma. That dharma, as laid out in the Gita, has been the ever-enduring foundation (*acyuta,* "ever-enduring," is Arjuna's first and last epithet for Krishna in the Gita) of this survivor religion. The eternal dharma renews itself in every generation. It doesn't do so by itself; it does so through the hard work of individuals.

I considered it my dharma, for example, to prepare this book.

BRAHMAN

The word *Brahman* does not refer to the same entity as *God.* *God* would be *Deva,* a word often used in the plural in the Gita. Brahman is (or rather, *neither is nor isn't*) a concept unique to Vedic thought, and I have discussed it in sections 3 and 4 of the foreword.

If I could have come up with a satisfactory substitute, I would have. Change the second *a* to an *i,* and *Brahman* becomes *Brahmin,* which is the word for a priest. Take off the *n* and *Brahman* becomes *Brahma,* the Creator of the universe, who is a God like Vishnu or Shiva and *not* the same entity as Brahman. This is important to know because both *Brahma* and *Brahmin* do show up elsewhere in the Gita.

If you choose to read this translation aloud, you should stress the second syllable of *Brahman.* For *Brahmin* and *Brahma,* stress the first.

AHIMSA, MAHATMA, KARMA, ATMAN

Three of these words have become familiar in English over the twentieth century.

Ahimsa and *mahatma* came in with Mahatma Gandhi and his ahimsa movement, which sought political revolution through nonviolent means. I thought it would be interesting for the reader to see where these words originated. It is one of Indian history's finest ironies that Gandhi built his nonviolent movement on a scripture imparted to explain why bloodshed, given the right casus belli, is worthwhile.

Karma has a general sense of your actions prompting a comeuppance—although Hinduism conceives of karma as carrying over to subsequent births, a residue. *Karma* and words derived from it are among the most frequent in the Gita. Most translators stick with *action,* but the Gita uses the word *karma* in several related senses. *Action* has an abstract feel that doesn't always mesh with the worldly connotation of *work,* or the vaguely moral feel of *works,* which comes from its use in Christian theological writing. Similarly, when Krishna refers to the moral residue or charge that comes with action, *karma* should stay *karma.* These variations in my usage—*action, work, works, karma*—track the nuances of context in the original.

This holds true for the word *atman* as well. Sometimes I follow the most common practice and use the term *self,* while in other instances, where the context deals with its unification with Brahman or its posthumous destiny, I keep *atman.*

I believe this practice—switching between two or more English words for the same Sanskrit word—has justification in Sanskrit itself, in which the same word can mean different things, and the same word contains, like undiffracted light, a spectrum of English meanings.

RUDRAS, ADITYAS, VASUS, AND OTHER BEINGS

Rudras, Adityas, Vasus, and other mythological beings show up mostly during the spectacular sequences of the Universal Form. Modern Hinduism does not focus on them nearly as much as classical Hinduism did. Most Hindus today experience these words as evocative proper nouns, much as poetry readers today experience the litanies of Hebrew proper nouns in Milton's *Paradise Lost*. I kept almost all of these references, except where a literal translation added some value, poetic or conceptual.

MAYA

Maya is another Sanskrit word familiar in America, if only because it is so frequently the first name of a fascinating woman. The common translation is *illusion,* implying metaphysical reality and the spectacular light and sound show surrounding it.

But we shouldn't imagine a Magician distracting us from a sleight of hand. His hands are in plain sight, as is the work of his hands. Maya relies on tendencies of human perception. Maya involves our mapping presence onto absence, and then mistaking that presence for all there is, and ignoring the actual Presence of the divine.

When I think of maya, I think of the Hermann grid optical illusion. On a grid consisting only of black squares surrounded by white space, we see flashing dots where emptiness intersects emptiness, where there is literally nothing to see. No matter what you tell your brain, you cannot not see those dots. The eyes chase them all but never catch one because focusing hard on a single dot makes it vanish instantly. It was never real.

And yet the word *illusion* isn't quite right. An illusion is deliberate; the illusionist does not want the illusion to be penetrated. In Hindu theology, any God is surrounded and hidden by maya, which he himself generates. It plays about his lips like a smile; it surrounds him in a perceptual cloud. He makes it, he maintains it, he hides within it—but he wants everyone to see through it.

And that is what the yogi aspires to do: to see through maya to reality. So maya is an illusion, yes, but its purpose is disillusionment; and disillusionment, in this context, is not a bad thing. In fact, it's the best possible thing of all. You can see why *illusion* breaks down when you plug it into the Gita. *Maya* is the only word that will do.

YOGA

While I am aware that the word *yoga* conjures, for most Americans, urban thirty-somethings in yoga pants on yoga mats deep-breathing and relieving stress, I had to keep this word as is. Commoditized, physical, studio-yoga has little to do with the Gita. At one point Krishna does describe the ideal meditation posture, but that's it.

Yoga comes from a root word meaning "to yoke," and yoking, or joining, comes up frequently: atman to Brahman, human self to divine self. Rare though they are in English, I retained the words *yoke, yoked,* or *yoking* wherever the Gita uses *yoga* or its related formations. I hope a waning of *yoke*'s agricultural connotation will allow for a rise, in the reader's mind, of its religious one. The sense of an ox yoked to the plow may well link up with the sacred Hindu image of the Cow: the yogi bowing and, like a beast of burden, taking on the yoke of discipline, duty, hard work, a kind of wooden garland.

A NOTE ON THE PROPER NOUNS

Before you begin the poem, a bit of context. A reader is advised to flip back to this section if any of the names or proper nouns get confusing. The first few pages contain a "Homeric catalogue" of allied princes and the names of conch-shell horns, a common feature of old heroic poetry. The Gita is actually a self-contained excerpt from the larger war epic *Mahabharata,* and these runs of proper nouns are the traces of that origin. You can take those proper nouns as word-music, which is what they are in the original; I assume you are here to focus on the Gita, so I won't launch into epic background on each of those names.

There are a few proper nouns, however, that a reader of the Gita needs to know. Most of these cluster in the first pages. Here they are, roughly in order of appearance.

DHRITARASHTRA

is the blind King whose words open the Gita.

PANDU

is King Dhritarashtra's late brother—so when Dhritarashtra refers, in the opening verses, to Pandu's sons, he's referring to his own nephews. The *Mahabharata* concerns a civil war, and Pandu's five sons are the "good guys," righteously fighting to get their kingdom back after they were cheated out of it in a dice game.

SANJAYA

is King Dhritarashtra's advisor. Sanjaya can see and hear across time and distance. In the blind King's throne room, Sanjaya recounts what happened on the battlefield of

KURUKSHETRA,

Kuru Field. This word is important, and not just because it's the second word, and physical scene, of the whole poem. Kuru was the remote common ancestor of the warring branches of the family. No matter whose son it is, Pandu's or Dhritarashtra's, they are all Kurus.

Dhritarashtra's one hundred sons, the Kauravas, are power-hungry, unscrupulous usurpers.

DURYODHAN,

the eldest son of King Dhritarashtra, delivers the archaic "Heroic Age" litany of warrior names in Session 1. (I have always thought that fitting because he is a very "might is right" sort of character.)

DRONA

trained both the Pandavas and the Kauravas in the art of war. It's to Drona that Duryodhan describes the gathered forces.

BHISHMA

is the illustrious great-uncle of the cousins, one of the most highly respected figures fighting on the Kaurava side.

is a son of Pandu, known for his great size. He is not to be confused with Bhishma. Finally,

KRISHNA *and* ARJUNA

are the two main characters of the Gita, the bulk of which is the dialogue between the son of Pandu, Arjuna, and his charioteer, Krishna. A respected and princely diplomat (not to mention an avatar of Vishnu), Krishna refrains from taking up arms in the civil war. Because he is Arjuna's best friend, though, he volunteers to drive Arjuna's chariot into battle.

Several epithets for these two figures occur over the course of the Gita. I made sure to translate the ones that matter, even when they sounded archaic; the Gita is part of an ancient epic, and traces of that *should* come through in a truly faithful translation. Sometimes I unpacked the epithet, incorporating the name itself to reduce confusion—as I did when preserving the brilliant epithet that links up the two Indian epics, *kapidhvaja,* "Monkey-bannered." Four syllables set up a parallel between Krishna's cherished fighter, Arjuna, and Rama's cherished fighter in the *Ramayana,* Hanuman. However, sometimes the epithets are there just to fill out the meter—"padding a line" wasn't considered a sign of insufficient skill back then. It is common practice in Homeric Greek, too. I assessed each epithet and made a conscious decision whether to preserve it.

Arjuna's epithets include

PARTHA *and* SON OF KUNTI.

Both of these epithets refer to Arjuna's mother. Such relationships are crucial to the drama of the poem, and these family-related epithets, especially in Session 1, dovetail with his anguished dilemma about whether or not to battle his relatives.

WEALTHWINNER

refers to Arjuna and is self-explanatory.

GANDIVA

is the name of Arjuna's bow.

BULL OF THE BHARATAS

is another epithet that refers to Arjuna, colorful and meaningful at once. Bharata was another one of Arjuna's ancestors. I preserved this one because Krishna happens to be talking about species at that point in the poem.

Several epithets of Krishna refer to details of his appearance or abstract traits. I have worked in references to Krishna's infallibility or his "bristling hair" where they seemed appropriate, but I could not bring myself to spell out Bristling-Haired One. The meaningfully deployed epithets I preserved were ones like

MADHU'S SCION,

which refers to Krishna's ancestry, in Session 1, at the same place where *Partha* refers to Arjuna's.

SLAYER OF MADHU

is another important descriptor of Krishna: This second Madhu was a demon slain by Vishnu, the God of whom Krishna is an avatar. The juxtaposition of these two Madhus, the relative and the slain demon, is intentional on the part of the Gita poet; Arjuna calls Krishna by this name while expressing his reluctance to slay his relatives.

~

In the translation, the tags that remind you who speaks ("Sanjaya said," "The Blessed Lord said," etc.) are carried over intact from the original text. They were placed there to do the same thing this brief note hopes to do: dispel any confusion. After all, dispelling confusion is why the Gita was sung in the first place.

Let's listen.

Godsong

Arjuna Despairs

King Dhritarashtra, the father of the cousins (the Kauravas) opposing Krishna and Arjuna, asks his visionary advisor, Sanjaya, what is happening on the battlefield. Sanjaya, who has the power to witness events without being physically present for them, narrates the action.

The action takes place on the battlefield of Kurukshetra. The two armies are in formation, facing off, ready to make war. Duryodhan, the leader of the Kauravas, addresses his military mentor, cataloguing the warriors on both sides.

Arjuna asks his friend and charioteer, Krishna, to park his chariot between the two armies. Surveying his extended family, he is overcome with panic and despair. He tells Krishna how he feels and how he has a horror of fighting his own relatives. Arjuna throws aside his weapons and sits down.

Dhritarashtra said,

On that field of dharma, Kurukshetra,
My sons and Pandu's
Mustered, wanting war.
What did they do, Sanjaya?   {1}

Sanjaya said,

Seeing the Pandava formation's
Vanguard, Duryodhan
Advanced toward his Master.
The words . . . the King is speaking. . . .   {2}

"Take a look at that army. How grand!
The sons of Pandu, Master, mustered
Under Drupad's son,
Your sharp-witted student.   {3}

The heroes here—great bowslingers!
Matches in a clash for Bhima and Arjuna,
For Yuyudhana and Virata
And Drupada in his great chariot.   {4}

Dhrishtaketu, Cekitana,
Kashi's heroic king,
Purujit, and Kuntibhoja,
And bull-necked Shaibhya,   {5}

Yudhamanyu with his spirited stride,
And courageous Uttamaujas,
Subhadra's sons and Draupadi's,
All in great chariots. . . .   {6}

Ours are excellent, too—better
Believe it, best of Brahmins!
Just so you can get a sense, I'll name
The marshals of my army: {7}

Your Lordship, Bhishma, Karna,
Battle-winning Kripa,
Asvatthama, Vikarna,
And Somadatta's son as well,   {8}

And many other heroes
Who give their lives up to my ends,
All specialists in war,
Armed to launch multiple strikes.   {9}

It has no measure, this force of ours
That Bhishma guards.
It measures up, that force of theirs
That Bhima guards. . . .   {10}

In all maneuvers,
Every one of you
At every station,
Keep guard over Bhishma!"   {11}

The eldest Kuru,
To make his grandson happy,
Sent up a lion roar
And searingly blew his conch shell.   {12}

At that, conch shells and kettledrums,
Cymbals, snare drums, bullhorns
Struck up all at once.
This sound became a tumult.   {13}

Standing fast behind the onrush
Of yoked white horses,
Madhu's scion and Pandu's son
Blew their divine conch shells.   {14}

Krishna, his hair bristling,
Blew Panchajanya. Wealthwinning Arjuna
Blew Godsgift. Wolf-bellied Bhima,
Fearsome in action, blew Paundra.   {15}

King Yudhishtir, Kunti's son,
Blew Neverending Victory.
Nakula and Sahadev
Blew Sweetsound and Gemblossom.   {16}

Kashi's king, the best of bowmen,
Shikhandin in his great chariot,
Dhrishtadyumna and Virata
And invincible Satyaki,   {17}

Drupad, Draupadi's sons,
Subhadra's great-armed son—
Your Majesty, they blew their conch shells,
Each his own and all together.   {18}

This hue and cry, King Dhritarashtra,
Tore through the hearts of your sons.
Of the sky and earth
The tumult made one thunder.   {19}

Under the banner of Hanuman, Arjuna
Scanned your sons in squadrons
Formed for the coming clash of arms.
Pandu's son held high his bow.   {20}

To a bristling Krishna, Arjuna
Spoke these words: "Ever-enduring one,
Station my chariot
Midway between the armies,   {21}

Just while I survey
The war lust of these squadrons.
Whose battle ardor wants
To make war with me?   {22}

I see them here, come together,
About to battle us. They want
A war to serve the evil
Mind of Dhritarashtra's son."   {23}

These were the words that Arjuna spoke
To Krishna where
Midway between the armies
He had stationed the chief chariot.   {24}

Faced with Bhishma and Drona
And all the rulers of the world,
Arjuna said, "Just look at this:
A Kuru Family gathering!"   {25}

Pritha's son could see them standing there:
Fathers and grandfathers,
Teachers, uncles, brothers,
Sons, grandsons, friends as well,   {26}

Fathers-in-law, kindhearted
Friends in both the armies,
All his relatives in close order.
The son of Kunti pondered them.   {27}

Pierced by infinite pity,
In despair, he said,
"Seeing this—my own people, Krishna—
Drawing close because they're dying to fight. . . .   {28}

My legs buckle
And my mouth dries up
And my body gets the shakes
And my hair stands on end!   {29}

Gandiva falls from my hand,
And my skin, it burns,
And I can't stand anymore,
And it's like it's . . . wandering, my mind. . . .   {30}

And I see omens, Krishna,
Inauspicious ones, and I
Can see no good will come
Of killing my own people in battle!   {31}

I don't want victory, Krishna,
Or a kingdom, or 'happiness.'
What's a kingdom to us, Cowherd?
What are pleasures, what is life?   {32}

The ones for whose sake we would want
Kingdoms, pleasures, happiness—
On a war footing here
They give up breath and wealth!   {33}

Teachers, fathers, sons,
Even grandfathers,
Uncles, fathers-in-law, grandsons,
Brothers-in-law . . . other relatives, too. . . .   {34}

Though they are out to kill me, Krishna,
I don't want to kill them—
Not for the kingship of three worlds!
How much less, then, for some ground?   {35}

Killing off Dhritarashtra's sons. . . .
What kind of joy would that be?
If we kill these hostile archers,
The evil's going to stick to us!   {36}

We just don't have the right to kill
Dhritarashtra's sons. Our own relatives!
If we really were to kill them,
How could we be happy, Krishna?   {37}

Even if greed so overpowers
Their thoughts that they can't see
How wrong it is to wreck a family,
How ruinous, to betray a friend,   {38}

Since when do *we* not know enough
To turn back from this sin?
Seeing clearly, Krishna, as we do
How wrong it is to wreck a family!   {39}

Wreck a family, the family's
Ancient laws vanish. Once its laws
Have vanished, lawlessness
Overpowers the whole family.   {40}

Lawlessness in power, Krishna,
The family's women grow corrupt.
The women once corrupted, Krishna,
The colors pour together.   {41}

Intermix, and it all goes to hell,
The family with the family's wreckers.
Their forefathers get debased,
Robbed of their ritual rice and water.   {42}

The wrongs of these family wreckers
Make the colors pour together—
Codes of caste, eternal
Family laws—obliterated! {43}

Men whose family laws
Have been obliterated, Krishna—
We've heard of this happening—
They dwell in hell forever! {44}

Ah—ach—what a great sin
We're hell-bent on committing!
So greedy for kingly pleasures
We're ready to kill our own people! {45}

If Dhritarashtra's sons, weapons in hand,
Were to kill me in battle
Weaponless and unresisting—
That would be easier for me! {46}

Having said this in the war zone,
Arjuna sat on the chariot seat,
Throwing down his bow and arrow,
His grief-stricken mind recoiling. {47}

Samkhya

Krishna berates Arjuna for cowardice, but Arjuna insists he doesn't want to attack his relatives and gurus. He admits he can't decide whether it's better for him to kill them or for them to kill him. This is the conundrum central to the Gita—where and whether to delimit empathy in a time of war—and it triggers Arjuna's first plea for instruction from Krishna. Immediately after begging for instruction, Arjuna says bluntly that he will not fight.

Krishna begins his teaching. He explains the indestructibility of the atman, its imperviousness to physical stimuli, and its transmigration from body to body. The logical conclusion of this is that Arjuna should not mourn anybody.

Krishna briefly takes up some more warrior-to-warrior arguments, pointing out how Arjuna, if he fights, will win either way—heaven if he dies, or worldly glory if he conquers. Differentiating deep understanding from showy ritualism, Krishna also throws in a few verses about hypocritical priests.

Returning to larger concepts, Krishna explains how Arjuna must focus only on the task at hand, not on the end results of it. The method for this is yoga, a multifaceted concept he will expand on over the course of the entire Gita. He speaks of how the intellect, "yoked" to yoga, can avoid the karma associated with action. This is another reason Arjuna should do his duty and fight.

Arjuna asks what such a person is like. Krishna spends much of the rest of the session describing the "steady mystic." The steady mystic attains Brahman, that is, his atman resorbs into its source. This state is nirvana—etymologically, the state of being "blown out," much as a candle might be.

Sanjaya said,
>   To him—seized this way with pity,
>   Tearful eyes cast down
>   And in despair—demonslaying
>   Krishna said these words.   {1}

The Blessed Lord said,
>   Where's this gutlessness coming from?
>   In a time of danger!
>   This is goddamned unbecoming.
>   This disgraces you, Arjuna!   {2}

>   Don't you be a coward, Partha—
>   It doesn't suit you!
>   Quit this base faintheartedness.
>   Stand up! Blaze your enemies!   {3}

Arjuna said,
>   How can I battle Bhishma
>   And Drona? Slayer of Madhu,
>   How can I attack with arrows
>   A pair so worthy of worship?   {4}

>   Better to go eating handouts here on earth
>   Than kill these great-minded gurus.
>   Killing these gurus out of a lust for gain
>   Would smear the food I feast on red.   {5}

>   No way to know which, for us, is of heavier importance:
>   Whether we should conquer them, or they should conquer us.
>   There they stand, facing us down—Dhritarashtra's sons.
>   If we were to kill them, we wouldn't want to live!   {6}

A guilty misery overcomes my whole being.
I ask you with my duty muddled in my mind:
Which would be better? Tell me for sure—
Me, your pupil—instruct me, I am at your feet! {7}

I just can't see what will take away
This sorrow drying up my senses
Though I gain an unrivaled and prosperous kingdom
On earth, or even preeminence over the Gods. {8}

Sanjaya said,
Having said this to Krishna,
Arjuna, the scorcher of foes,
Said, "I will not fight,"
And went silent. {9}

To him in his dejection, King,
Midway between the armies,
Krishna—as if about to start
Laughing—said these words. {10}

The Blessed Lord said,
You've mourned for those you shouldn't mourn.
What words of wisdom in your speech!
Scholars mourn no body,
Empty of breath or full of breath. {11}

Never have I not existed,
Nor you, nor these human rulers.
Nor will any of us ever
Not exist from here on out. {12}

What this body embodies
Just as it takes on boyhood, youth, and age
Takes on another body, too.
A sage is not confused by this. {13}

Brushes with matter, Arjuna,
Causing cold or heat or pain or pleasure
Come and go, ephemeral.
Suffer to endure them, Arjuna.   {14}

A bull of a man like you
Who does not tremble at them,
A sage the same in pain and pleasure—
He is set for immortality.   {15}

What is *un*real cannot come to be.
What is real cannot *not* be.
Two conclusions. Those who see true
See the truth in both.   {16}

Indestructibility: Be aware
It spreads through all this.
Destroying this imperishable part
Is something no one can accomplish.   {17}

They say these bodies that embody
Indestructible, immeasurable
Eternities must have an end.
So *fight,* Arjuna!   {18}

Someone who imagines this a killer,
Someone who believes that this is killed—
Neither of them knows
This cannot kill and cannot *be* killed.   {19}

It is not born and does not die at any time
And, having come to be, will never cease to be.
Birthless, undying, constant, before time, this
When killed inside the body is not killed.   {20}

A man who knows the indestructible,
Eternal, birthless, imperishable *this*—
In what way, Partha, does he
Cause the killing? Who is it he kills?   {21}

Casting off his worn-out clothes,
A man takes hold of others. That
Is how the self, embodied, casts off worn-out
Bodies, moving on with new ones.   {22}

This is what the weapons do not cut.
This is what the fire does not burn.
This is what the water does not wet,
Nor does the storm wind make it wither.   {23}

No way to cut or burn
Or wet or wither this.
This is undying, all-pervading, stable.
This is immovable and everlasting.   {24}

This is unmanifest, it's said,
Unthinkable, immutable.
And so, in that way knowing this,
You should not mourn.   {25}

Mighty-armed Arjuna,
Even if you think this
Born forever or forever dead,
You should not mourn for this.   {26}

For what is born a death is sure
And sure a birth for what is dead.
Over this inevitable meaning
You are not to mourn.   {27}

Unmanifest at their beginnings, beings
Manifest midway, their ends
Unmanifest again.
Arjuna, why complain about it?   {28}

A wonder is what someone sees in this,
"Wonderful!" declares another,
"A wonder!" is what still another hears,
But even hearing of this, no one really knows this.   {29}

This, embodied, is invulnerable
In everyone forever, Arjuna.
And so for all these beings
You should not mourn.   {30}

Seeing the dharma proper to you,
You should not tremble.
A warrior finds nothing better
Than a dharmic battle!   {31}

If by accident they happen
On the open gate of heaven,
Happy the warriors, Partha,
Who get in on such a battle!   {32}

If you do not undertake this
Dharmic combat, then in
Dereliction of your duty,
In dishonor, you will take on sin.   {33}

People will forever tell
The tale of your dishonor.
For a high-born man, dishonor
Is worse than death.   {34}

Great chariot-fighters will believe
You shirked the skirmish, scared.
Among the ones who thought so much
Of you, you'll come to seem a lightweight;   {35}

Foes who scorn your prowess
Will call you many
Unspeakable words.
What sorrow's worse than that?   {36}

Either you'll be killed, and get to heaven,
Or you will conquer, and enjoy the earth—
So stand up, son of Kunti,
Emboldened into battle!   {37}

Making pleasure and pain, loss and gain,
Victory and defeat the same,
Yoke yourself to battle: That
Is how you will not take on sin.   {38}

This, the Samkhya school described to you:
Hear it now, a yogic mindset.
Yoked to such a mindset, Partha,
You will throw off karmic bondage.   {39}

Here no effort goes to waste.
You never find yourself backsliding.
Even a little of this dharma
Guards against great danger.   {40}

The self-willed mindset
Is at one here, Arjuna.
Many-branched, and endless, really,
Are irresolution's many minds.   {41}

Such flowery words they declaim, these
Ignoramuses! Delighting,
Partha, in the letter of the Veda,
Saying there is nothing else.   {42}

Desire in their natures, heaven-bent
And holding out rebirth as work's fruition,
They act out many different rituals
With the goal of glut and grandeur.   {43}

Hooked on glut and grandeur,
Their thinking carried off
By that, they're never granted
Meditation's self-willed mindset.   {44}

Three gunas are the subject of the Vedas:
Of these three gunas, Arjuna, be free,
Beyond dichotomies, in truth forever fixed,
Never getting, never hoarding, self-possessed.   {45}

A well when water's flooding
In from every side is
Worth as much as all the Vedas
To the knowing Brahmin.   {46}

The action alone is your mandate,
Never the fruits at any time.
Never let the fruits of action goad you.
Never get attached to your inertia.   {47}

Fixed in yoga, do your work
Relinquishing attachment, Wealthwinner.
In success or failure, stay the same.
It's said that equilibrium is yoga.   {48}

Action is by far beneath
An intellectual yoga. Wealthwinner,
Seek refuge in the intellect.
Fruition's a pitiful motive.   {49}

Yoked, the intellect can leave behind
Both good and evil karma here.
So yoke yourself to yoga!
Yoga is finesse in action.   {50}

Intellects, when yoked, relinquish
Fruits that come of action. Wise men,
Released from the bonds of rebirth,
Go to a place of no more pain.   {51}

When your intellect has passed on
Through delusion's thicket,
What you've heard and what you haven't
Heard yet will disgust you.   {52}

When your intellect, its interest
In holy hearsay fallen off,
Stands fixed in meditation—
That's when you'll attain to yoga.   {53}

Arjuna said,
How is the steady mystic spoken of?
Steady in meditation, Krishna,
Steady in vision—how does he speak?
How does he sit, how does he move?   {54}

The Blessed Lord said,
When he leaves behind all the desires,
Partha, passing through his mind,
Self-contained and self-contented,
He is called a steady mystic.   {55}

In unhappiness, his mind unworried,
In happiness, his longings gone,
His passion, fear, and anger vanished,
Vision steady: He is called a sage.   {56}

Unattached on all sides, neither
Celebrating what he gets nor hating it,
This or that, lucky or unlucky:
His mysticism stands fast.   {57}

When he draws the senses
In from what they're sensing,
All together, just like tortoise limbs,
His mysticism stands fast.   {58}

Things of the senses turn off
The one who fasts inside the body,
But not their *flavor*. Even flavor,
Once he sees the Highest, turns him off.   {59}

Even a striver, son of Kunti,
Even a perceptive man—
The senses, riled, carry
Off his mind by force!   {60}

Arresting all of them,
Yoked, with me his zenith,
Let him sit, his senses checked.
His mysticism stands fast.   {61}

When a person contemplates things,
An attachment to them takes birth.
Attachment gives birth to desire.
From desire, rage is born.   {62}

From anger comes delusion,
From delusion, a wandering memory,
From a wandering memory, loss of the intellect,
And from the loss of intellect the loss of you.   {63}

Unyoked from hate and passion,
Moving senses past things,
Self-restrained, the governed atman
Approaches serenity.   {64}

From serenity is born
The surcease of all sorrows.
Serenity of thought at once
Stabilizes intellect.   {65}

No intellect, in one who isn't yoked.
No yoking, no development.
Someone undeveloped cannot be at peace.
For someone not at peace, what happiness?   {66}

When the roving senses
Overrule the mind, they carry
Off its mystic knowing
Like a windboat over water.   {67}

Someone who draws his senses
Back from what they sense on all sides—
Great-armed Arjuna,
His mysticism stands fast.   {68}

In what is night to all the species,
A man restrained will stay awake.
When other species stay awake,
That is night for the sage who sees.   {69}

Filling up but motionless, the ocean
Stands there while the waters enter:
When desires enter him, he gains in peace,
Unlike a lover of desires.   {70}

A man who moves on,
Forsaking all desires, free of lust,
No "me" and "mine," and no self-seeking:
He goes on to peace.   {71}

This state: Brahman. Once he attains it,
Partha, he is not deluded.
Fixed inside it even when his time ends,
He reaches, in Brahman, extinction.   {72}

Karma

Arjuna points out that even though Krishna has extolled an intellectual steady state, he is goading Arjuna to violent action. Krishna explains that everyone has to act in some way. You can do nothing, but you cannot not do. Even inaction is a kind of action and bears a karmic charge.

Here Krishna introduces the notion of sacrifice. He draws an implicit parallel between the Vedic sacrifice—the most sacred set of actions possible—and everyday actions in the conflict-ridden world. The latter can be identical with the former.

Sacrifice implies reciprocity between human beings and Gods. This mutual fostering, Krishna explains, in turn fosters social order.

Krishna sets up an analogy between himself and Arjuna. Just as Krishna sustains the universe, Arjuna must sustain a dharmic society. To do this, both of them must act. Yet these actions must be carried out with detachment, and with the focus on the task itself. Krishna encourages Arjuna to see action as something that his atman isn't even doing: Actions are performed by the gunas, which belong to "nature"—in a sense, it's just Arjuna's physical nature doing these things, not his immortal atman.

Krishna adds a few words about the importance of following this doctrine. He also insists that everyone should know his or her own dharma and act accordingly.

Arjuna asks what drives people to do evil actions. Krishna speaks of desire and anger, and how they can obscure the understanding. He finishes with a martial metaphor, exhorting Arjuna to combat and kill desire.

Arjuna said,

> If you think intellect
> Better than action, Krishna,
> Why would you yoke me
> To this horrific action?   {1}

> With muddled talk
> You seem to confuse my intellect.
> Tell me for sure by which one
> I can attain the highest good.   {2}

The Blessed Lord said,

> Long ago in this world
> I proclaimed a dual dedication:
> Knowledge yoga, for the Samkhyas;
> Active yoga, for the yogis.   {3}

> Not by shirking actions does a man
> Enjoy a state beyond all karma,
> Nor by mere renunciation
> Does he reach perfection.   {4}

> No one for an instant ever really
> Stands there doing nothing.
> Gunas, born of nature, make
> *Everyone* do things, even if unwilling.   {5}

> Some deluded self who quells
> His powers of action, sitting while
> His mind remembers what he's sensed—
> He's called a hypocrite.   {6}

> When he quells his senses with his mind,
> Arjuna, and undertakes
> An active yoga with his powers of action,
> Unattached, he is supreme.   {7}

You must do the proper action.
Action is much better than inaction.
Your body couldn't even manage
Its ongoing functions if it didn't act.   {8}

This world is bound by karma save
For works whose aim is sacrifice.
With *that* aim, son of Kunti, carry out
Your action, from attachments freed.   {9}

Issuing sacrifices and mankind together,
The Father of Mankind once said,
"May you proliferate with this.
May this be the cow that fulfills your desires.   {10}

By this may you foster the Gods,
And may the Gods foster you.
Fostering each other,
You will attain the highest good."   {11}

Fostered by the sacrifice, the Gods will
Surely grant the feast you wish for.
Whoever feasts but doesn't offer
Back these gifts is just a thief.   {12}

Eating what remains of sacrifices,
Saints are freed of all their guilt.
The wicked, cooking for their
Own sake, feast on sin.   {13}

Creatures come to be through food.
The Rain God is the source of food.
The Rain God comes to be through sacrifice.
Of sacrifice, the source is action.   {14}

The source of action is Brahman;
Brahman arises from the indestructible.
That's how sacrifice establishes forever
Brahman pervading all.   {15}

Whoever doesn't turn the wheel
That started turning here—
In malice and in sensuality,
Arjuna, he lives in vain.   {16}

Should a man be self-
Delighting, self-
Satisfied, and self-content,
He finds no need to act.   {17}

Neither action nor inaction
Has a purpose for him here,
And nor does he depend on any
Being for a purpose.   {18}

So, unattached forever,
Do the work that must be done.
A man who does his work while
Unattached attains the highest.   {19}

Consider: Janaka and others
Gained, through works alone, perfection.
If only so the world can hold
Together, you should work.   {20}

What the best of men does,
That the rest of men do.
The standard *he* sets,
People follow.   {21}

In three worlds, there is not one thing
I need to do, nor anything
I haven't won I have to win,
But I move into action anyway.   {22}

If I never moved myself to work—
And tirelessly, Partha—
Human beings everywhere
Would follow in my tracks.   {23}

These worlds would drop off
If I didn't do my work,
And I would make a muddle.
I would kill off species.   {24}

While the unwise work from their attachment
To action, Arjuna, a sage
Should work without attachment,
Longing to hold the world together.   {25}

A sage should not disrupt the minds
Of those unknowingly attached to action.
Conscientious, yoked, he should
Encourage them in all their actions.   {26}

Actions everywhere are done
By nature's gunas, yet the self,
Deluded egoist, imagines
"I'm the one who does them."   {27}

But one who knows the truth that
Gunas and actions both partake of
Thinks, "The gunas act on gunas."
Arjuna, he doesn't get attached.   {28}

Fools the gunas have deluded
Get attached to what the gunas do.
They do not know the whole, but knowers
Of the whole should not unsettle them.   {29}

Renouncing all your works in me,
Your metaself in mind,
Freed of fantasies, no sense of "mine,"
Your fever broken, *fight*.   {30}

Human beings who practice
My doctrine constantly,
Full of faith and never sneering—
They, too, are freed from karma.   {31}

But those who sneer at this,
Not practicing my doctrine,
All their knowledge muddled—know them
To be lost and mindless.   {32}

Each one strives according to
His nature, even men of knowledge.
Beings follow nature:
What use repressing it?   {33}

In everything the senses sense
Passion and hatred reside,
Both of them, waylayers:
You mustn't go into their territory.   {34}

Better your own dharma, botched,
Than someone else's dharma practiced well.
Better death in your own dharma!
Another's dharma carries danger.   {35}

Arjuna said,
> Then what drives a man—
> Even when he doesn't wish it,
> Krishna—to commit a sin
> As if yoked to it by force?　　　　　{36}

The Blessed Lord said,
> This desire, this anger—
> Their source, the Power guna,
> Great its appetite and great its evil.
> Know this for the enemy it is.　　　　{37}

> As smoke envelops fire,
> As dust envelops a mirror,
> As amnion envelops embryo,
> So this envelops that.　　　　　　　{38}

> The knowledge of the knower
> Is enveloped by this eternal enemy
> Whose body is desire, Arjuna,
> A fire hard to fill.　　　　　　　　{39}

> Its base, they say, is in the senses,
> Mind, and intellect. With these
> It dupes this atman in the body,
> Enveloping its knowledge.　　　　　{40}

> So subdue the senses first,
> Bull of the Bharatas,
> And then go kill this sinful
> Destroyer of knowledge and judgment.　{41}

> They say the senses are the height—
> But higher than the senses is the mind,
> And even higher than the mind is intellect.
> What's higher than the intellect is *this*.　{42}

So, learning what's beyond all learning,
Supporting yourself by your self,
Kill with your mighty arms the foe, so
Hard to charge, whose body is desire.   {43}

Renounce Through Knowledge

Krishna details the lineage of his wisdom, tracing it back to an ancient God of sunrise. Arjuna is baffled by this. Gradually, Krishna has started singing from a divine perspective—but Arjuna reverts to thinking of Krishna as a friend of the same age. So he asks how this is possible.

Krishna explains reincarnation and how, from time to time, he takes birth to reestablish dharma. People can transcend rebirth by understanding him.

Freedom from death and rebirth means freedom from karma; freedom from karma involves understanding the nature of action (see Session 3). So Arjuna should do his work on earth to maintain dharma, just as his forebears did (and just as Krishna, having taken birth, is doing).

Krishna describes the ideal man of action, with a focus on his detachment, and how he "accrues no guilt." Such a yogi's work in the world takes on the nature of sacrifice—an offering to the Gods. Krishna dwells on the different kinds of sacrifice.

He goes on to praise yogic knowledge and how it dissolves karma. The yogi's "actions are through yoga / Renounced."

Again he ends with a martial metaphor, urging Arjuna to use this knowledge as a sword to cut out his self-doubt.

The Blessed Lord said,
>This imperishable yoga
>I proclaimed to Vivasvat;
>Vivasvat explained it to Manu;
>Manu told it to Ishkvaku.   {1}

>Each one got it from another,
>And so the royal seers knew this.
>After a long time here, this yoga,
>Arjuna, was lost.   {2}

>That ancient yoga
>I proclaim to you today
>Since you're my friend, devoted to me.
>This really is the highest mystery.   {3}

Arjuna said,
>Your birth was afterward,
>The birth of Vivasvat, earlier. . . .
>How should I understand this?
>*You* proclaimed it at the start?   {4}

The Blessed Lord said,
>Many are my bygone
>Births—and yours, too,
>Arjuna. I know them all,
>But you don't know them.   {5}

>Birthless though my deathless self is,
>Lord of beings though I am,
>I stand above my own nature
>And come to be through my own maya.   {6}

From time to time, when dharma
Drops exhausted, Arjuna,
And when adharma is insurgent:
It's then that I create myself.   {7}

To protect the righteous,
To destroy wrongdoers,
With a mission to establish dharma,
I come to be in era after era.   {8}

When one who knows my birth and works
In their divine reality
Lets his body go, he does not come
To be reborn. He comes to me.   {9}

Their passion, fear, and anger vanished,
Filled with me, with me their refuge,
By austerity and knowledge purified,
Many have gone on to become me.   {10}

In whatever way they shelter
In me, I reward them.
People everywhere,
Partha, follow in my tracks.   {11}

Expecting actions to succeed,
They sacrifice here, to the Gods,
And swiftly in the human world
Their actions come to be successful.   {12}

I created four castes that
Apportion works and gunas.
Though I am their maker,
Be aware I do not do things.   {13}

No karma smears me.
No fruit of action tempts me.
Actions do not bind whoever
Understands me this way.   {14}

Knowing this, your forebears,
Seeking freedom, did their work.
Now you, too—do your work
Just as your forebears in the past did!   {15}

"What is action? What is inaction?"
About this, even poets are deluded.
I will explain to you what action is,
And knowing it will free you from misfortune.   {16}

What action is you have to understand;
You also have to understand wrong action;
Inaction, too, you have to understand.
The way of karma is impenetrable.   {17}

In action perceiving inaction,
And in inaction, action,
A human being is wise
And yoked. The work he does is whole.   {18}

Someone whose every endeavor excludes
Desire and calculation, karma
Burned up in the fire of knowledge—
Wise men call him learned.   {19}

Giving up attachment to the fruits of action,
Ever contented, independent,
Even when he goes ahead with action,
He isn't doing anything at all.   {20}

Without vain hopes, his thought and self
Restrained, acquisitiveness given up,
He accrues no guilt, performing
Actions only with his body.   {21}

Content with what he gets by chance,
Beyond both opposites, his envy gone,
The same in both success and failure,
Even when he acts, he isn't bound.   {22}

For the unattached and free
Who fix their minds in knowledge,
Action, working toward
Sacrifice, dissolves entirely.   {23}

The offering is Brahman. Brahman
Pours out Brahman into the fire of Brahman.
He can attain Brahman
By meditating on the workings of Brahman.   {24}

Some yogis carry out
Their sacrifices to a God
While others sacrifice the sacrifice
Itself into the fire of Brahman.   {25}

Others pour their senses, hearing first,
Into the fires of restraint.
Others pour what they perceive, sounds first,
Into the fires of the senses.   {26}

Still others offer all the actions
Of their senses and their breath
Into the fire of yogic self-
Restraint, which knowledge kindles.   {27}

Some offer things while others offer
Austerity or offer yoga.
Disciplined seekers, making keen vows,
Study on their own and offer knowledge.   {28}

Some offer, into the breath out, the breath in;
Others, into the breath in, the breath out.
They check the goings, out and in, of breaths,
Intent on extending the breath . . . .   {29}

Still others who restrain their diet
Offer, into the breath in, the breath in.
All of them know what sacrifice is.
Sacrifice destroys what stains them.   {30}

Eating the nectar-sweet remains of sacrifice,
They go on to Brahman, the everlasting.
As for those who do not sacrifice, if *this* world
Isn't theirs, how can the other be?   {31}

So many kinds of sacrifices
Spread before Brahman's mouth:
Know them all as born of action.
Knowing this will set you free.   {32}

Better than the sacrifice of things:
The knowledge sacrifice.
All works without exception
Consummate in wisdom.   {33}

Know that if you bow low,
Ask questions, and serve them,
Knowers who can see reality
Will direct you toward knowledge.   {34}

Son of Pandu, once you *know* this,
You won't go back to these delusions.
All creatures you will see
Within yourself and then in me. {35}

Even if you were the most
Sinful of any sinner,
In the boat of knowledge
You would cross beyond transgression. {36}

As a kindled fire
Makes ashes out of kindling,
So the fire of knowledge
Makes ashes out of every action. {37}

You can find no purifier here
That's quite like knowledge:
Someone who perfects himself through yoga
Finds it in the atman, given time. {38}

With that his highest aim, senses restrained,
His faithfulness gains knowledge.
Knowledge gained, he goes
In no time to the highest peace. {39}

The ignorant and faithless
Skeptic perishes.
Not this world, not the one beyond,
No happiness for any skeptic! {40}

A man whose actions are through yoga
Renounced, whose knowledge has cut out
His doubt, who's self-possessed:
No actions bind him, Arjuna. {41}

So, with the sword of knowledge,
Cut out this self-doubt! It is born
Of ignorance and lodges in your heart.
Resort to yoga, Arjuna! Stand up!   {42}

Renounce Through Works

Arjuna voices, again, his confusion over Krishna's contradictions—specifically what Krishna means by actions renounced in yoga. Is Arjuna supposed to "do" yoga, or renounce action?

Krishna favors action over renunciation, though he concedes that both have their benefits. He refers to the Samkhya school of thought as an example of the way of renunciation—but he insists that what he teaches doesn't conflict with that teaching. Yoga is a way of acting and renouncing action at the same time. The yogi pulls this off by renouncing the fruits of action. He escapes all karmic consequences while continuing to do the hard work of dharma in the world.

Krishna speaks of how the world looks from this enlightened perspective. Once the yogi attains extinction in Brahman, he sees all things and people as fundamentally equal because they are fundamentally the same. That is nirvana, a state of bliss and peace, and Krishna describes it at length.

Arjuna said,
>Renouncing action. Yoga.
>You praise one, then the other,
>Krishna. Of the two, which one
>Is better? Tell me definitely.   {1}

The Blessed Lord said,
>Both renunciation and an active
>Yoga work the greatest good,
>But of the two, an active yoga
>Is better than renouncing action.   {2}

>Know that an eternal renunciant
>Is one who neither hates nor covets,
>Neutral toward things opposed.
>Blithely he gets free of bondage.   {3}

>"Samkhya and yoga are separate!" So
>The childish proclaim, but not the scholars.
>Rightly rooted in even one,
>You find the fruit of both.   {4}

>The place that followers of Samkhya
>Get to, yogis also reach.
>Samkhya and yoga are one.
>To see this is to see true.   {5}

>Renunciation, if devoid of yoga,
>Is painful to attain.
>Yoked to yoga, any wise man
>Reaches Brahman in no time.   {6}

>Yoked to yoga, ego purged,
>Ego vanquished, senses vanquished,
>His self becomes the self of every being.
>Even when he acts, it doesn't smear him.   {7}

"I'm not doing anything"—so thinks
A yogi who's aware of what is real
Whether he's seeing, hearing, touching, smelling,
Eating, walking, sleeping, breathing,   {8}

Talking, defecating, grasping,
Opening the eyes, closing the eyes . . .
"The senses orbit what they sense."
That is his conviction.   {9}

Placing his actions in Brahman,
Giving attachment up, he does his work,
And he is smeared no more by sin
Than is a lotus-leaf by water.   {10}

With body, mind, and intellect,
Or even only with the senses,
The yogis, giving up attachments,
Purify themselves by doing works.   {11}

A yoked man, letting fruits of action go,
Attains the ultimate peace,
But *un*yoked, acting on his lusts,
He clings to fruit, in bondage.   {12}

Renouncing all acts with the mind,
Sitting happily, the one inside
The body rules that nine-gated City
And neither acts nor actuates.   {13}

Neither activity nor actions
Does the Lord create in people, nor the link
Between the action and its fruit:
It's personality that spurs them.   {14}

The Omnipresent doesn't take on
Anybody's sins or good deeds.
Ignorance, deluding people,
Covers up their knowledge. {15}

For some, though, knowledge can destroy
Their ignorance about themselves.
Their knowledge, like the sun,
Illuminates the Highest. {16}

Their intellects on that, on that their atmans,
Their basis that, and that their highest goal,
They go on to a point of no rebirth.
Knowledge shakes off evils. {17}

A wise and cultured Brahmin,
A cow, an elephant,
A dog, a man who *cooks* dog:
Scholars see them all the same. {18}

Here on earth, those minds abiding
In equality will beat rebirth. Because
Brahman is faultlessly egalitarian,
It's in Brahman that they abide. {19}

You shouldn't rejoice to get what you prize
Or shudder to get what you don't.
With steady intellect and no delusions,
A knower of Brahman abides within Brahman. {20}

Atman detached from what he touches,
Finding joy within himself,
Brahman and atman yoked through yoga,
He gains a joy that cannot be destroyed. {21}

Arjuna, pleasures born of touch
Are really wombs of pain.
They start and end. A sage
Does not delight in them.   {22}

If a man not free yet of his body
Can withstand the shocks
That come of lust and anger here,
He is a yoked, a happy man.   {23}

His happiness within, his ease
Within, and hence his light within,
This yogi goes up to extinction
In Brahman, be*comes* Brahman.   {24}

Seers, self-restrained, attain
Extinction in Brahman,
Their sins depleted, doubts cut out,
Rejoicing in the good of all.   {25}

For seekers who know themselves—
Uncoupled from their rage and lust,
Restrained in thought—extinction
In Brahman lies close.   {26}

External stimuli shut out,
Focus kept between the eyebrows,
Inhalation, exhalation
Moving, balanced, in the nostrils,   {27}

Senses, mind, and intellect controlled,
Desire, fear, and anger gone,
A hermit headed high for freedom
Frees himself forever.   {28}

Knowing me—the one who eats
What sacrifices heat, Great Lord
Of all the world, a friend to every
Species—he will go in peace.

{29}

Concentrate

K rishna continues with an extended portrait of the man of action who has renounced the fruits of action. This includes psychological traits, like equanimity and self-restraint, as well as practical details of how he sets up a place for meditation. The end of yoga is an insight into the unity of all beings, divine, human, and nonhuman.

Arjuna, skeptical about this portrait, points out how fickle the mind is, but Krishna insists that state is possible, however difficult.

Granted that it is difficult, what happens to someone who tries yoga, makes some progress, but ultimately fails to reach Brahman? Krishna assures Arjuna that, in yoga, no work is lost. The process takes many births, and each well-lived life wins a rebirth that makes it easy to resume the quest.

The Blessed Lord said,

Whoever does the work that's to be done
Without relying on the fruit of it
Is a renunciant and yogi, not
Someone without a fire or a rite.   {1}

What they call renunciation—know that
To be yoga, son of Pandu.
Without renouncing his ambition,
No one becomes a yogi.   {2}

For a sage aspiring to ascend in yoga,
It's said the method is the work.
For the one who has ascended yoga,
It's said the method is serenity.   {3}

When he clings no more
To sensual things or actions,
His ambitions all renounced, then
It's said he has ascended yoga.   {4}

You should uplift the self by the self.
You should not abase yourself.
Only the self is the self's friend,
The self alone the self's enemy.   {5}

The friend of the self is the self of one
Whose self is vanquished by the self;
For one whose self is not, the self,
Inimical, behaves like any enemy.   {6}

Self-vanquished, pacified,
The highest self will stay composed
In cold and heat and pleasure and pain
As well as honor and dishonor.   {7}

Full of knowledge and discernment,
Standing on a peak, his senses vanquished,
Yoked: That's how a yogi's said to be,
A clod, a rock, and gold the same to him. {8}

He is distinguished by fair-mindedness
To benefactors, friends, and foes,
To those who sit apart, or stand in the middle,
Haters and family members, saints and sinners. {9}

The yogi always ought to yoke
Himself while staying reticent,
Alone, restrained in mind and self,
Without ambitions or possessions. {10}

Setting up a firm seat
In a clean place for himself,
Not too high and not too low, with cloth,
Antelope hide, and kusha grass on top: {11}

There, sitting on that seat
And single-mindedly restraining
Thoughts and senses, yoked
In yoga, he should purify himself, {12}

Holding torso, head, and neck upright,
Motionless, steady,
Staring at the tip of his own nose,
Not looking in any direction. {13}

Pacified, his fear gone, yoked and steadfast
In the vow to seek Brahman,
His mind controlled and thinking of me,
He should sit with me his zenith. {14}

Yoking himself this way forever,
The yogi with a quelled mind
Goes on to peace, the highest extinction.
He stands at one with me.   {15}

Never eating too much,
Never eating absolutely nothing,
Not habitually oversleeping, not
Staying awake, either: That is yoga.   {16}

Yoga kills the pain of any body
Disciplined in diet and diversion,
Disciplined when doing work,
Disciplined in sleep and wake.   {17}

When he settles in the atman
With his thoughts in check,
Free of longings, free of all desires:
That, they say, is when he's "yoked."   {18}

The way a lamp that stands in no wind doesn't flicker:
That's a memorable simile about
The yogi with his thoughts controlled,
Yoked to the yoga of the self.   {19}

When his thought is curbed,
Checked by yogic service,
The self that sees itself
Fulfills itself.   {20}

Transcendent happiness,
Grasped by the intellect, transcends
The senses. One who knows it
Stands, unwaveringly, in reality,   {21}

And once he gains it, he imagines
No other greater gain than that.
It stabilizes him. Not even
Heavy sorrow shakes him.   {22}

Let it be known: What we call yoga
Unyokes you from the yoke of pain.
Yoga should be practiced confidently
By a mind that isn't downcast.   {23}

Letting go, without exception,
Desires born of motives,
Over the rabble of his senses
His mind's control complete,   {24}

Bit by bit he should withdraw,
Intellect in a steady grip, his mind
Made up to stand fast with the atman.
He should not think of anything at all.   {25}

Wherever it may wander off
(This skittery, unsteady mind!)
From there he ought to draw it back
And lead it to the master atman.   {26}

The sinless yogi with a peaceful
Mind, his passions pacified,
Arriving at the highest
Happiness becomes Brahman.   {27}

Always yoked this way,
The yogi, all his sins gone,
Touches Brahman with ease
And gains transcendent bliss.   {28}

The self in every creature,
Every creature in the self:
The atman yoked in yoga
Sees identity at all times.   {29}

Whoever sees me everywhere
And sees, in me, the all—
I'm not lost to him,
And he's not lost to me.   {30}

A yogi who abides in oneness
Worships me abiding in all beings.
However else his way of life
May be, he lives in me.   {31}

The yogi who sees all identities,
Their happiness, their suffering,
As metaphorically his own
Is thought to be the highest.   {32}

Arjuna said,
This yoga you profess
To be an equilibrium—Krishna,
I don't see a steady state for this
Because of fickleness.   {33}

The mind is really fickle, Krishna—
Riotous, strong, stubborn!
I think its restraint is as hard
To achieve as the wind's.   {34}

The Blessed Lord said,
No doubt the restless mind
Is hard to hold back,
But practice and dispassion
Can hold it, Arjuna.   {35}

For someone with no self-control,
Yoga, I believe, is hard to gain,
But still, it's possible for self-will
To attain by means of striving.   {36}

Arjuna said,
If an unruly mind arrives at faith,
But having strayed from yoga
Hasn't come to yogic consummation,
Which way does he go, Krishna?   {37}

Doesn't he fall from both worlds,
Effaced like a cloud? Lost,
Krishna, with no solid footing,
Confused on the path of Brahman?   {38}

You can efface this doubt of mine
Completely, Krishna.
No one but you steps forward
To efface this doubt.   {39}

The Blessed Lord said,
Partha, he is lost
Neither here nor there above.
No one who does good work, son,
Has to walk a hard road.   {40}

After reaching the worlds of the virtuous
And dwelling there for endless years,
A lapsed yogi is born again
In a pious and prosperous home.   {41}

Or else he may be born into
A family of learned yogis.
A birth of this kind in the world
Is even harder to attain,   {42}

For there he gains the gathered
Wisdom of his prior bodies.
He strives from there once more
For consummation, son of Kuru.   {43}

Prior progress bears him onward,
Even against his will.
Even the wish to know of yoga
Goes beyond the word *Brahman*.   {44}

With perseverance, mind in check,
A yogi wholly cleansed of guilt
And over many births perfected
Goes on to the highest goal.   {45}

The yogi goes beyond ascetics.
The learned, too, he's thought to go beyond.
The yogi goes beyond the actors in a rite.
So be a yogi, Arjuna!   {46}

Of all these yogis, one
Whose inmost self has come to me
And worships me with full faith—
He's the most united with me.   {47}

Know and Discern

Krishna shares how to know him in his entirety, both his lower nature and his higher nature. His lower nature encompasses both physical "nature" and an individual's psychological "nature." His higher nature is spiritual and cosmic, and he gives examples of how he is the essential, defining element of things. While he originates the gunas, he stays independent of them.

Krishna expresses how dear his "knower" is to him. Yet he does not despise or exclude people who worship other Gods in other ways, and he rewards them according to their due.

People, as soon as they are born, grow susceptible to delusions about reality, for example, the delusion that the world is rife with opposite qualities (instead of its all being Brahman). After warning Arjuna about these delusions, Krishna assures him that people who strive to know him will come to know him whole.

The Blessed Lord said,

Mind fixed on me, with me your refuge,
Yoked in yoga, Partha,
You can know me whole,
Without a doubt. Now listen how.   {1}

Knowledge with discernment—
I'll tell you both and leave out nothing.
Once you know them, there is nothing
Further to be known here.   {2}

Humans, thousands of them . . . . Hardly
Anybody strives toward perfection.
Even among perfected strivers,
Hardly anybody really knows me.   {3}

Earth, water, fire, wind,
Air, mind, intellect,
And sense of self: These
Divide my nature eight ways.   {4}

But these are lower. Know my *highest*
Nature to be different, great-armed
Arjuna. It's the living spirit
That undergirds the universe.   {5}

Understand this
Womb of every being.
The universe entire
I originate and I dissolve.   {6}

There is nothing else
That's higher than me, Arjuna.
All this is strung on me
Like pearls on a thread.   {7}

I am the flavor in water, Arjuna.
I am the shining forth of sun and moon.
I am the *Aum* that hums in every Veda,
The sound in the air, the manhood in men.   {8}

I am the sacred fragrance in the earth.
I am the brilliance in the flame,
The life in every species.
I am the rigor of ascetics.   {9}

Know me, Partha, for the everlasting
Seed of every species.
The wisdom of the wise is me,
The brilliance of the brilliant, me,   {10}

The strength of strong men, also me,
Of lust and passion free. In every
Species, Bull of the Bharatas,
I'm the lust that doesn't contravene the dharma.   {11}

The Pure, the Powerful, the Dark:
Be aware these ways
Of being come from me,
But I'm not in them. They're in me.   {12}

These three ways of being,
Gunas, braid the whole world—
Which, deluded, does not recognize
I am above them, and above decay.   {13}

This maya of mine is divine.
Made of gunas, it is hard to go beyond.
Only people who resort
To me transcend this maya.   {14}

Fools and criminals, the basest
Men, do not take refuge in me.
Their knowledge carried off by maya,
They resort to a demonic way of being. {15}

Four kinds of beneficent men
Worship me, Arjuna:
The sufferer, the questioner,
The driven seeker, and the knower. {16}

Of these, a knower—always yoked,
Exclusively devoted—is the best.
To a knower, I am very
Dear, and he is dear to me. {17}

All these may well be exalted; still,
I think of the knower as myself.
His atman yoked, he's fixed
On me alone, the highest path. {18}

At the end of many births,
The knower shelters in me.
"Vasudeva is all"—so thinks this
Hard-to-find mahatma. {19}

Ravished of knowledge by this or that
Desire, some take refuge with other Gods.
They resort to this or that religious rule,
Ruled by their own natures. {20}

Whatever form someone's
Devotion wishes to revere,
To each for each I grant
A faith that does not waver. {21}

Yoked to his faith and wishing
To propitiate that,
From that he gets his wishes—
Granted, in fact, by me.   {22}

For the small-minded, though,
Fruition is fleeting.
Worshippers of Gods go on to Gods,
But devotees of me will come to me.   {23}

The unwise think of me as fallen
From unmanifest to manifest,
Not knowing how my higher being
Is undying, unsurpassed.   {24}

Enveloped by my yogic magic,
I do not shine for all.
This deluded world can't recognize me
As unborn, undying.   {25}

I know the passed on,
And the passing,
And beings yet to be,
But not a one knows me.   {26}

Since yearning and aversion surge,
Because dualities delude,
All beings fall into delusion,
Arjuna, at birth.   {27}

People whose works are pure,
Whose sins are at an end,
Freed of duality's delusion
Worship me with solid vows.   {28}

Strivers who depend on me
For freedom from old age and death
Know Brahman completely
And metaself and karma whole.   {29}

They know *me,* the metabeing, *me,*
The metagod and metasacrifice.
Yoked in thought, they know me even
At the hour of their passing.   {30}

Brahman the Imperishable

K rishna has just used some specific theological terms, and Arjuna asks him what they mean, as well as how to know him at the time of death.

Krishna offers a brief definition of each term, then speaks of how the last thoughts of a human being are crucial in determining how he is reborn—or whether he is reborn at all, since it is possible to enter Brahman after death. Krishna speaks of how to die like that.

Most beings are reborn, however. This holds true of both the individual and the collective: One creature's repeated births and deaths have an analogy in all creation's repeated geneses and dissolutions. Krishna redefines Day and Night on a cosmic scale to illustrate this kindred cyclicity.

Only a yogi can choose whether he will be reborn or not, and Krishna describes the two paths between which the yogi gets to choose.

Arjuna said,

What's this *Brahman*? What's *metaself*?
What's *action*? Highest Man,
How would you describe the *metabeing*?
The *metagod*—what do they say that is?   {1}

Who or what in this body
Is the *metasacrifice,* Krishna?
And how, at the time of passing on,
Is the quelled atman to know you?   {2}

The Blessed Lord said,

Brahman is the highest indestructibility.
The self's own nature, called the metaself,
Makes beings become who they are.
Creativity is known as action.   {3}

The metabeing is the perishable creature.
The human spirit is the metagod.
Arjuna, best of the body-borne,
The metasacrifice is me, embodied here.   {4}

Whoever, when his time ends,
Gets free of his body
While remembering me goes on
To become me. There's no doubt about this.   {5}

Whatever being he remembers
At the end, when he gives up his body—
That is where he goes, becoming
That being, son of Kunti, every time.   {6}

Therefore at all times
Remember me, and fight.
Devote your mind and intellect
To me. You'll come to me without a doubt.   {7}

With his thinking yoked to yogic
Practice, never straying,
Contemplation takes him
To the highest human godhood.   {8}

Remembering the ancient poet, the ruler
Smaller than an atom, the supporter
Of all, the image unimaginable—
Suncolored, beyond dark—   {9}

At the time of his passing on, mind motionless,
Yoked to devotion with the strength of yoga,
Lifesbreath entering right between the eyebrows,
He approaches this highest human godhood.   {10}

Ascetics, free from passion, enter
What knowers of the Vedas call the Indestructible:
Wanting it, they follow lives that seek Brahman.
Briefly I will speak to you about that step.   {11}

All the gates secured,
Mind shut inside the heart,
Lifesbreath set inside the head,
Seated steadily in yoga,   {12}

Reciting *Aum,* the sole syllabic
Brahman, remembering me,
He goes out, goes on to the way
Beyond, his body left behind.   {13}

His never-deviating mind
Remembers me always.
For such a yogi, always yoked,
Partha, I'm easy to reach.   {14}

Approaching me, mahatmas
Gone to the highest perfection
Do not get reborn
In suffering's ephemeral house. {15}

Up to Brahma's realm
People return again, but son
Of Kunti, once they come to *me,*
They never find themselves reborn. {16}

Brahma's one Day stretches
For a thousand aeons. After
A thousand aeons, Night ends. People
Who know this know the Day and Night. {17}

From the Unmanifest, manifestations
All proceed, come Day;
Come Night, they dissolve,
Known from then on as unmanifest. {18}

This crowd of beings—
Becoming, becoming, dissolved
Unwillingly come Night—
Will come to be again, come Day. {19}

Beyond this being is another. More
Unmanifest than the Unmanifest,
Eternal in all creatures,
It doesn't perish when they perish. {20}

What is unmanifest they call
Imperishable, the way beyond.
Attaining it, no one returns.
My highest home is there. {21}

Devotion, never deviating, gains
The highest human godhood, Partha,
That expands through all of this.
All beings stand inside it.   {22}

The time that yogis, when they
Pass on, go to places of
Return or no return—of this time,
Arjuna, I will speak.   {23}

Fire, brightness, day, the waxing moon,
Six months the sun is moving northward:
Passing on from there, the knowers
Of Brahman go to Brahman.   {24}

Smoke, night, the waning moon,
Six months the sun is moving southward:
From there the yogi, taking on
The brightness of the moon, returns.   {25}

These two ways, light and dark,
Are thought eternal in the universe.
By one he goes on, never to return,
While by the other he returns again.   {26}

Knowing these two paths
No yogi is deluded.
So be at all times
Yoked in yoga, Arjuna.   {27}

Vedic study, sacrifice, austerity,
And charity mete out fruits of merit.
The yogi, knowing all this, goes beyond them
To the highest state: his original one.   {28}

Royal Wisdom, Royal Secret

Krishna, seeing that Arjuna does not scoff at him, promises to tell him a secret: He declares himself the origin of the cosmos and its living species, and says that he has originated and dissolved these many times. This great claim may be hard to believe about someone in a human body, and Krishna contrasts the "deluded people" who scorn him in his human body (the Kauravas among them) with the mahatmas who worship him through devotional work or the pursuit of knowledge.

Krishna expands on his own divine qualities and roles—one of which is as the universal recipient of worship, regardless of whether that worship is performed by "devotees of other Gods." He accepts the offering of anyone striving with devotion. Because he is the same in all beings, anyone, including sinners and socially subordinate people, can achieve his state of being.

The Blessed Lord said,

But since you aren't scoffing,
I'll proclaim to you the utmost secret,
Knowledge together with discernment.
Knowing it will free you from misfortune.   {1}

A royal wisdom, royal secret,
This—the highest purifier,
Understood at first sight, dharmic,
Easy to enact, imperishable.   {2}

Men who put no faith
In dharma don't attain me,
Arjuna, returning
To death and rebirth in a circular course.   {3}

I expand this whole
Cosmos, unmanifest in form.
All species have their stations in me,
But I don't stay in them,   {4}

And nor do species stay in me—
You see my lordly yoga!
The sustenance but not the state of being,
I myself cause beings to be.   {5}

Consider: As the great winds,
Though they go all over,
Stay forever in the sky,
All species stay in me.   {6}

All species, son of Kunti,
Come into my nature when an era's
Made extinct. Then, at an era's
Genesis, I reproduce them.   {7}

Established in my own nature,
I reproduce, again and again,
This entire throng of species
Powerless in my natural power.   {8}

And yet these actions
Do not bind me, Wealthwinner.
Though seated in these actions
I sit apart, detached.   {9}

With me for overseer, nature
Breeds what moves and doesn't move.
This motive, son of Kunti,
Makes the world revolve.   {10}

Deluded people scorn me
In my haven of a human body,
Ignorant of my higher being
As the great God of Being.   {11}

Vain their hopes and vain their works,
Their knowledge vain, devoid of thought,
Their monstrous and demonic natures
Abide in their delusion.   {12}

Mahatmas, Arjuna, abiding
In a godly nature, worship
Single-mindedly, aware
Of being's imperishable source.   {13}

Constantly glorifying me,
Striving, solid in their vows,
Bowing down, devoted to me,
Always yoked, they worship.   {14}

Sacrificing through the knowledge-
Sacrifice, still others worship me
As one and multiple,
Manifold, facing everywhere. {15}

I am the rite, I am the sacrifice,
I am the offering, I am the herb,
I am the mantram, I am the ghee,
I am the fire, I am the libation. {16}

I am the father of the universe,
Its mother, founder, grandfather,
The not yet known, the purifier, the syllable *Aum,*
The Rig, the Sama, and the Yajur Veda, {17}

Path, scaffold, master, witness,
Home, sanctuary, friend,
Genesis, dissolution, base,
Treasury, imperishable seed! {18}

I heat up; I hold in
And I send out the rain.
I am deathlessness and death,
Real and unreal, Arjuna. {19}

Thrice-wise drinkers of Soma, rinsed of sins,
Worship me with sacrifices in the quest for heaven.
The virtuous get to the world of the chief of Gods.
They feast in the sky on the Gods' divine delights. {20}

Having enjoyed the expansive world of heaven,
Their virtue spent, they enter the world of mortals,
And thereby following the triple dharma,
They come and they go, wishing their wishes and
　　getting them. {21}

Men who sit close by me,
Yoked perpetually,
Their thoughts on no one else—
I bring them what they need for yoga. {22}

Even the devotees of other Gods
Who sacrifice with faith
Sacrifice to me as well,
Though not according to the rules. {23}

All their sacrifices
I alone enjoy and master.
They don't recognize
The truth of me. And so they fall. {24}

Devotees of Gods go to the Gods;
Devotees of forefathers go to forefathers;
Devotees of spirits go to spirits.
Those who sacrifice to me are sure to go to me. {25}

A leaf, a flower, fruit, water
Offered, with devotion,
By a striving atman: That
Devoted offering I eat. {26}

Whatever you do, whatever you eat,
Whatever you offer, whatever you give,
Whatever you burn for, son of Kunti,
Do that as an offering to me. {27}

Freed from karmic bondage,
From its lucky or unlucky fruit,
Yoked to the yoga of renunciation,
Set free, you will come to me. {28}

I am the same in all beings.
There is none I hate or favor.
Those who worship me devotedly
Are in me, as am I in them. {29}

Even if a man who does wrong
Worships me, devoted to no other,
He should be considered good
And right in his resolve. {30}

Swiftly he becomes a dharmic man
And goes to everlasting peace.
Arjuna, understand that
No devotee of mine is lost. {31}

Partha, by taking refuge in me,
Women, merchants, even peasants
Though from sinful wombs
Go the highest route. {32}

How much easier it is for virtuous
Brahmins, for devoted royal seers!
Having gotten to this brief, unhappy
World, devote yourself to me. {33}

Mind on me, devoted to me,
Sacrifice to me and bow to me.
Yoking yourself like this, you'll come to
Me, your passage beyond. {34}

Expansive Glories

Krishna's self-revelation continues, prompted by his love for his friend. Arjuna asks to be told the ways the divine manifests in the world.

Krishna agrees, pointing out that he will limit himself to the main ones—as he must, being endless. Although present in all beings, divinity shines through most clearly in the preeminent one of each kind. Krishna describes himself in an extended litany that includes natural phenomena, abstract entities, animals, Gods, and people. At the end of it, he downplays his own litany—his sustaining power in the world is just "one fraction" of himself.

The Blessed Lord said,

Hear my highest word again,
Arjuna. Because I wish
Your welfare, I will tell it
To you, the one I love.   {1}

No crowd of Gods or visionaries
Knows how I have come to be.
I am the source of Gods
And visionaries everywhere.   {2}

Whoever knows me—no birth, no
Beginning, the world's great Lord—
He alone is an enlightened mortal,
From all his sins released.   {3}

Knowledge, enlightenment, intellect,
Honesty, patience, composure, control,
Pleasure, pain, becoming and ceasing to be,
Fear and fearlessness,   {4}

Fairness, ahimsa, contentment,
Austerity, charity, infamy, fame . . . .
Beings are the many ways
They are because of me.   {5}

Seven ancient visionaries,
Four Manus, too,
Who peopled this planet:
I birthed them with my mind.   {6}

Whoever knows this truth
About my yogic immanence
By unswerving yoga
Will no doubt unite with me.   {7}

I bring it all to be,
And from me, all evolves.
The wise and meditative
Think this as they worship me.   {8}

Thoughts on me, living me and breathing
Me, each one enlightening another,
Always discussing me, they find
Contentedness and joy.   {9}

I give them intellectual yoga
By which they come to me
Constantly yoked
In loving worship.   {10}

Compassionately I destroy
The Dark of their unknowing.
From my place in their own beings,
I shine a lamp of knowledge.   {11}

Arjuna said,
Highest Brahman, highest home,
Highest purifier—*You*—
Spirit eternal and divine, Primal
God, birthless, all-pervading. . . .   {12}

So all the seers call you—
The divine seer Narada,
Asita Devala, too, and Vyasa.
And you yourself say so.   {13}

All this you tell me, Krishna, blessed
Krishna, and I believe it's true.
Nobody knows your revelation,
Not the Gods and not the demons.   {14}

You alone know yourself
Through yourself—the Highest Man,
Benefactor of beings, Lord of beings,
God of Gods, universal master!   {15}

Tell me, please, leaving nothing out,
Your own divine manifestations,
Your immanent forms in the planets
You steep and inhabit.   {16}

How should I know you, yogi,
And always think of you?
What are your many ways of being many?
How do I *think* you, blessed one?   {17}

Speak of yourself in detail, Krishna,
Your immanence, your yoga.
The nectar never
Slakes my hearing.   {18}

The Blessed Lord said,
Listen! I will tell you
My own divine manifestations—
Only the main ones, Arjuna,
Since my extent is endless.   {19}

I am the atman, Arjuna,
In every creature, my seat the heart.
I, the beginning of beings,
Am their middle as well as their end.   {20}

Among Aditi's sons, I am Vishnu,
Of lights, the sun, radiant.
I am Marici of the hurricanes.
Of night stars, I am the rabbit moon.   {21}

Of Vedas, I am Sama Veda,
And of the Devas, Indra.
Among the senses, I am the mind.
In creatures, I am sentience, {22}

And I am Shiva of the Gods who roar.
Of spirits and fiends, I am the God of Money,
Of elemental Gods, the purifying Fire.
Of mountain peaks, I am Meru. {23}

Partha, know me for the chief
Of priests, Brihaspati.
Of marshals, I am Skanda, God of War;
Of bodies of water, the ocean. {24}

Of visionaries, I am Bhrigu,
Of sounds, the soul syllable *Aum*.
Of prayers, I am prayer's repetition;
Of fixed things, Himalaya, home of snows. {25}

Of all trees, I am the Sacred Fig;
Of godly seers, Narada,
Of heavenly musicians, Chitraratha,
And of perfected wise men, Kapila. {26}

Of horses, I am Utchayshravus—
Know that I was born of nectar.
Of royal elephants, I am Airavata,
Of men, a King of men. {27}

Of missiles, I am the lightning bolt;
Of cows, the wish-fulfilling Kamadhenu.
I am the God of desire, begetting.
Among the serpents, I am Vasuki; {28}

Among the snakes, Ananta, endless;
Among seagoers, Varuna.
Of forefathers, I am Aryaman,
Of quellers, the God of death. {29}

Of demons, I am Prahlada;
Of reckoners, I am Time.
Among the beasts, I am the King of Beasts,
Among the birds, Garuda. {30}

Of scourers, I am the wind;
Of men who bear arms, Rama.
Among sea monsters, I am the crocodile.
I am the Ganga of rivers. {31}

Creation's start and end
And middle, Arjuna, I am:
Of sciences, the science of the atman,
Among logicians, inference. {32}

Of letters, I am *A*,
Of compound words, the kenning.
I, alone indelible, am Time;
I am the Basis, my faces everywhere. {33}

I am death, seizing all.
I am the genesis of futures.
Of women, I am Fame, Wealth, Speech,
Memory, Wit, Constancy, Forgiveness. {34}

I am the Brihatsaman of chants,
I am the Gayatri of meters;
Of months, the ninth, the Deer's Head;
Of seasons, spring, a mine of flowers. {35}

I am the cunning in hustlers,
The brilliance in the brilliant.
The win is me, the grit is me.
I am the truth in what is true.   {36}

Of the Vrishnis, I am Krishna,
And of the sons of Pandu, Arjuna.
Of wise men, I am Vyasa,
Of poets, the poet Ushanas.   {37}

I am the ruler's rod of rebuke,
The counsel of the conquest-keen.
I am the silence of secrets,
The knowledge of those in the know.   {38}

In every creature, Arjuna,
I am the seed.
Nothing that moves, nothing that doesn't
Exists except through me.   {39}

There is no end to my divine
Manifestations, Arjuna.
I have proclaimed through these examples
My manifest sweep.   {40}

Whatever being is manifestly
Glorious and powerful:
Realize, in every case,
Its source is a share of my splendor.   {41}

Yet this multiplicity of knowledge . . . .
Arjuna, what is it to you?
As I stand here, I'm sustaining
This whole world with one fraction of myself.   {42}

Envision the Universal Form

A rjuna now presses Krishna for the most direct revelation, asking to see his friend in his Universal Form.

Krishna reveals himself—at first a little overhastily; he remembers that Arjuna will require a "divine eye" to see what he is being shown.

Once this eye is granted, Arjuna witnesses Krishna's Universal Form. This form combines multiplicity and unity. He sees a vast hybrid of human bodies and celestial bodies ("the moon and the sun for your eyes"), a pictorial analogy that expresses how individual atmans and Brahman are really the same.

Arjuna's emotions range from awe and wonder to terror, particularly when he sees the warriors around him, getting eaten up by enormous mouths. He asks the Form to speak to him.

The Form identifies itself as Time and exhorts Arjuna to fight.

Arjuna joins his palms, bows, and stutters praise. He also begs forgiveness for having treated Krishna as a human friend for so many years. His joy is mixed with terror, and he begs to see Krishna in the form he recognizes from before.

Krishna obliges and instructs Arjuna not to fear. Arjuna calms down. Krishna emphasizes, twice, that the usual religious behaviors—ritual sacrifices, charity, austerities—are not the way to access this vision. What is required is what Arjuna has: personal devotion.

Arjuna said,

Out of kindness to me
You've told me, in words, the highest
Secret, known as the *metaself*.
This delusion of mine has left me.   {1}

Beings, becoming and bygone,
As well as your imperishable greatness—
Krishna of the lotus eyes,
I've heard you detail both to me.   {2}

The way you say you are, Highest
God, is how I wish
To see you, Highest
Man: in your divine form.   {3}

If you think it's possible
For me to see that, God-
Prince of yoga, let me see
Your imperishable self.   {4}

The Blessed Lord said,

Look at me, Partha—forms,
A hundred, more, a thousandfold,
Divine multiplicities,
Multiple colors and shapes!   {5}

Look at the Adityas, Vasus, Rudras,
Two Ashvins, the Maruts, too—
Look at wonders, Arjuna,
Many never seen before!   {6}

Look now at the cosmos whole, at everything
That moves and everything that doesn't,
In my body standing here as one
With whatever else you wish to see!   {7}

But you can't see me
With this, your own eye. . . .
I'll give you a *divine* eye.
Look at my majestic yoga!   {8}

Sanjaya said,
    Having said this, King,
    Yoga's great Lord Vishnu
    Showed to Arjuna
    His highest, his majestic Form.   {9}

Many a mouth and eye,
Many a glimpse of wonder,
Many divine decorations,
Divine the many weapons raised,   {10}

Divine the wreaths and clothes he wears,
Divine perfumes and oils,
Made of every marvel, God
Unending, facing everywhere at once!   {11}

If in the sky a thousand suns
Were all at once to rise,
Such radiance would match
The radiance of this mahatma!   {12}

The cosmos whole
Divided many ways
Arjuna saw there stand as one
In the body of the God of Gods!   {13}

Then, shot through with amazement,
Hair standing on end,
Arjuna, bowing his head to the God
And pressing his palms together, said,   {14}

Arjuna said,

> I see the Gods, O God, in your body,
> And every species of creature crowded together,
> And Brahma the Lord in the lotus asana seated,
> And all of the seers and celestial serpents! {15}

> With so many arms—bellies—mouths—eyes—
> I see you in every direction—unending Form!
> No end and no midpoint, I see no beginning to you,
> Universal God, Universal Form! {16}

> You with your crown and your mace and your chakram,
> Massive with brilliance and everywhere flaring!
> I see you, though it is hard to see you, whole,
> Your solar flares radiant beyond measure. {17}

> You are unchanging, the highest unknown,
> You the highest treasury of all this,
> You the imperishable guard of eternal dharma,
> The everlasting human spirit: This is my belief. {18}

> No beginning, no middle, no end, infinite power
> With infinite arms, the moon and the sun for your eyes—
> I see you—your mouth the blaze that eats the offering,
> Heating all this with your own brilliance. {19}

> You alone in every direction pervade
> This space between the earth and heaven.
> Seeing this marvelous, monstrous form of yours,
> The three worlds, Mahatma, are trembling! {20}

> Over there, crowds of Gods enter you, some of them
> Terrified, joining their palms as they hymn you.
> Siddhas and visionaries praise you, abundant
> With their praise, whole congregations saying *Hail!* {21}

Rudras and Adityas, Vasus and Sadhyas,
Vishves and Ashvins, the Maruts, the Drinkers of Steam,
Crowds of Gandharvas, Yakshas, Siddhas, Asuras—
All behold you in astonishment.   {22}

Your mighty form—its many mouths and many eyes,
Its many mighty arms, many thighs and many feet,
Many bellies, many harrowing tusks—seeing this,
The worlds are shaking—so am I!   {23}

A multicolor blaze that touches the sky,
Mouths agape, and vast and blazing eyes—
I see you, and my inner self is shaking!
I find no calm or courage, Vishnu!   {24}

Seeing these harrowing tusks of yours
In mouths that resemble the fires of time,
I have lost my direction, I can't get to shelter!
Lord God, home of the moving world, have mercy!   {25}

Over there . . . they enter you. . . . Dhritarashtra's sons,
All of them, along with crowds of earthly rulers,
Bhishma and Drona, and Karna, that son of a charioteer,
Together with ours . . . over there . . . even our main
   warriors. . . .   {26}

Swiftly they enter your mouths
With those fearsome, those harrowing tusks!
Some of them I see with mashed heads
Stuck between your teeth!   {27}

As the rapids of several rivers
Run to the ocean, so
The heroes of the human world
Enter your flaming mouths.   {28}

As moths to their destruction swiftly swarming
Enter blazing flame,
The worlds to their destruction enter
Your mouths, too, swiftly swarming. {29}

Your flaming mouths lick up and swallow
Planets whole on all sides. Vishnu,
Your fierce rays, filling this entire
Universe with brilliance, burn it up! {30}

Tell me who you are, fearsome Form—
Namaste to you, best of Gods! Mercy!
I want to understand you, primordial one!
I just don't understand your workings! {31}

The Blessed Lord said,
I am Time. I make worlds die.
I have come here to annihilate worlds.
All these warriors, stationed in opposing ranks:
Even without you, they will cease to be. {32}

So stand up. Get your glory.
Beat your enemies. Enjoy a thriving kingdom.
I have struck them down already.
Archer, simply be my instrument. {33}

Drona, Bhishma, Jayadratha,
Karna, and others, too. War heroes. Killed
By me. Now *you* kill. Do not tremble!
Fight! You'll beat your rivals in the joy of battle! {34}

Sanjaya said,
On hearing these words of Krishna's,
The crown prince joined his palms, trembling,
And made another bow. Kneeling, he spoke
To Krishna in a terror-struck stutter. {35}

Arjuna said,

The cosmos rejoices, Krishna, and rightly so,
Pleased to praise you. Rakshasas, fearful,
Run away in all directions. Crowds
Of perfected beings bow to you.   {36}

And why shouldn't they bow to you, Mahatma?
Greater than Brahma, the first creator,
Lord God without end, the universe's home,
Imperishable you, the being unbeing beyond!   {37}

You are the first Deva, the ancient human spirit,
The highest treasury of all the universe.
You are the knower, the unknown, the highest home.
You spread across the universe, your form unending.   {38}

You are Vayu, Yama, Agni, Varuna, the rabbit moon,
Father of creatures, great-grandfather, you!
Namaste! Namaste! Make it a thousand times,
And once more, and again, namaste, namaste!   {39}

Namaste before and behind you!
Namaste, All, from all around!
Infinite valor, measureless power, you!
You complete it all. Therefore you *are* all.   {40}

Whenever—rashly, thinking you a friend—I've said,
"Hey, Krishna! Hey, son of Yadu! Hey, friend!"
Carelessly, or even if affectionately,
Not knowing the majesty of you,   {41}

And if I disrespected you—for the sake of a joke,
Or at play, or in bed, or sitting and dining,
Alone, or before the eyes of others—boundless, ever-
Enduring Krishna, I beg your forgiveness for that!   {42}

Father of the world, of all that moves and all that doesn't,
Its guru most venerable, worthy of worship,
No one compares to you. How could another be greater,
Unrivaled Original, anywhere in three worlds?   {43}

And so I bow, I lay my body flat,
Asking for mercy from you, praiseworthy Lord.
As father would son, or friend would friend,
As lover would lover, please, God, bear with me.   {44}

I rejoice to have seen what has never been seen
Before, but terror shakes my mind!
God, let me see you again in that form—
Have mercy, Lord God, home of the moving world!—   {45}

With a crown and a mace and a chakram in hand.
I want to see you *that* way.
Become the form with four limbs,
Oh you with a thousand arms, a universe of shapes. . . .   {46}

The Blessed Lord said,
By my grace and my yogic power, Arjuna,
I have shown you this highest of forms.
It's made of light, primordial, cosmic, endless.
I have shown it to no one before you.   {47}

Not by Vedic sacrifice or study, not by gifts,
Not by doing rites or harsh austerities—
No one in the human world can see this Form.
Only you. The hero of the Kurus.   {48}

Do not tremble. Do not be confused.
Now that you have seen this fearsome Form of mine,
Be free of fear again, and in high spirits.
Now look at me in *this* form.   {49}

Sanjaya said,
  Krishna, having said this to Arjuna,
  Showed his own form, as before. Becoming
  Gentle and wondrously handsome again,
  The mahatma calmed the frightened one.   {50}

Arjuna said,
  Krishna, I see this human,
  This gentle form of yours.
  I am composed now, my mind
  Returning to its nature.   {51}

The Blessed Lord said,
  This Form of mine you saw
  Is hard to see.
  Even Gods are always
  Hoping for the sight of it.   {52}

  Not the Vedas, not austerities,
  Neither charity nor sacrifices
  Make it possible
  To see me as you saw me.   {53}

  It's possible, Arjuna,
  Through focused devotion alone
  To know and witness my
  Reality and enter me.   {54}

  Someone who does my work, depends
  On me, devotes himself to me, attachments
  Let go, no enmity for any being:
  Arjuna, he comes to me.   {55}

Devote Yourself

Arjuna wants to know which is the best form of yoga, personal devotion or worship of an abstract God. Krishna says that both ways can attain him, but the pursuit of an abstract understanding is harder.

In fact, Krishna is interested in making it as easy as possible. He offers a descending scale of difficulty: steady mental focus, the practice of yoga, working for holy causes, or merely taking refuge in his power and exerting self-control.

Krishna goes on to describe the serene impartiality of the devotee.

Arjuna said,
> Who knows yoga best—
> Devotees perpetually
> Yoked to you, or worshippers
> Of the eternal Unmanifest?   {1}

The Blessed Lord said,
> Worshippers who fix their minds on me,
> Continually yoked to me,
> Initiated in the highest faith:
> I think of them as yoked the closest.   {2}

> But those who honor
> Changeless unmanifest mystery,
> Unthought-of, all-pervading,
> The fixed, immovable pinnacle,   {3}

> The mob of their senses quelled,
> On all sides evenhanded: They
> Attain me, too, rejoicing
> In the betterment of every creature.   {4}

> The strain is greater on those minds
> That fix on the Unmanifest.
> To get to the Unmanifest,
> A body goes through pain.   {5}

> But those who lay down all their works
> In me, exalting me,
> Whose yogic focus does not wander
> When they worship me—   {6}

> Such people, Arjuna,
> I salvage soon enough
> From the ocean of death and rebirth.
> I absorb their thought.   {7}

Keep your mind on me alone,
Have me absorb your intellect,
And from then on, without a doubt,
You will reside in me.   {8}

Or, if you just can't keep on
Thinking steadily of me,
Then practice yoga, Arjuna,
To seek and reach me.   {9}

If you cannot even practice that,
Make my works your highest goal.
Merely doing work for me,
You will reach perfection.   {10}

If even *this* is something that you can't
Quite do, take refuge in my power.
Let go of all the fruits of action
And act with self-control.   {11}

Better than practice: knowledge. Better
Than knowledge: meditation. Better
Than meditation: letting go the fruits
Of action. Once you've let go—instant peace.   {12}

With malice toward none,
Friendly and compassionate,
Neither selfish nor self-serving,
The same in pain and pleasure, patient,   {13}

A yogi constantly content
Is self-controlled and rooted in resolve.
His mind and intellect to me entrusted,
My devotee is dear to me.   {14}

The world does not repulse him,
And he does not repulse the world.
Freed of glee and pique, of fright
And worry, he is dear to me.   {15}

Expecting nothing, pure, adroit,
Sitting apart, his trembling gone
And all initiatives relinquished,
My devotee is dear to me.   {16}

He doesn't rejoice, he doesn't hate,
He doesn't mourn, he doesn't yearn.
Letting go of good and bad,
Full of devotion, he is dear to me.   {17}

The same to enemy and friend,
The same in honor and dishonor,
In heat and cold and pain and pleasure
The same, free of attachment,   {18}

Alike when praised or censured, silent,
Content with anything at all, at home
Anywhere, steady-minded: Such a man,
Full of devotion, is dear to me.   {19}

I speak this sweet, immortalizing
Dharma. Those who honor it,
Offering faith, exalting me—
They are extremely dear to me.   {20}

The Field and the Knower of the Field

Arjuna asks about sentience and substance, as well as "the Field" and "the Knower of the Field."

Krishna explains that the Field is the body, and he goes into detail about its components. He describes the qualities of the Knower, and then he describes what the Knower knows, Brahman. So the Knower knows the Field, or his own body, by getting to know Brahman.

The other part of Arjuna's question, concerning sentience and substance, receives its answer as well: Krishna locates sentience (*Purusha*—see the Listener's Guide to this session) inside the material body. Through the body, sentience experiences the three gunas, which are also born of substance or material nature.

This way of understanding experience keeps the atman at a remove from physical action. This, in turn, keeps it from being "smeared" by physical actions—including, though Krishna never makes this explicit, warfare.

Arjuna said,
    Substance and Sentience, the Field
    And Knower of the Field,
    Knowledge, and what is known:
    I want to learn of these.   {1}

The Blessed Lord said,
    This body, Arjuna,
    Is called the Field. Someone
    Who knows this is the Knower of
    The Field. So say the experts on this.   {2}

    Know me for the Knower of the Field
    In every Field. To know the Field
    And know the *Knower* of the Field:
    That's what I consider knowledge.   {3}

    Hear me out about the Field now,
    Briefly—what it is and what it's like,
    What its adaptations are and why,
    Who its Knower is, and what his powers are.   {4}

    Seers have sung it many ways
    In many different hymns
    And lines from Brahmin sutras
    Unquestionably reasoned out.   {5}

    The major elements, the sense
    Of self, the intellect, the Unmanifest,
    The ten sense organs and the mind,
    The five fields where the senses graze,   {6}

    Desire, hatred, pleasure, pain,
    Constitution, courage, consciousness:
    This is, in summary, the Field
    Described with adaptations.   {7}

No pride, no affectation,
Ahimsa, patience, honesty,
Service to your teacher, purity,
Steadiness and self-restraint,   {8}

Disinterest in the objects
Of the senses, selflessness,
Perceiving the evils of birth, death,
Old age, disease, and pain,   {9}

Detachment (none of this clinging
To a son, house, wife, and all that),
Constant equanimity about
Events desired or undesired,   {10}

Devotedness to me that never
Strays, no other yoga,
Secluded places your resort, with no
Excitement in a mass of people,   {11}

Knowledge your goal, kept constantly in sight,
Knowledge of metaself, of what is *real*—
This, I say, is knowledge.
Ignorance is what isn't this.   {12}

I will proclaim what must be known.
Knowing it, you take on deathlessness,
Beginningless Brahman, the highest.
They say it neither is nor isn't.   {13}

Everywhere its hands and feet,
Everywhere its eyes, heads, faces,
Everywhere its ears, worldwide,
Everything-enveloping it stands,   {14}

Illuminating gunas with all the senses
Yet free of all the senses,
Unattached yet buttressing it all,
Devoid of gunas, yet enjoying gunas,   {15}

Outside and inside beings,
Those that move and those that don't . . . .
Subtlety makes this hard to know!
It stands far off and close by.   {16}

Though in all creatures undivided,
The Vishnu who nourishes species,
Known as their devourer and evolution,
Dwells in them *as if* divided.   {17}

They say this is the light of lights as well,
Beyond the darkness—knowledge,
What there is to know, the goal of knowing,
Seated in the hearts of everyone.   {18}

So that is how they're summarized: the Field,
Knowledge, and what there is to know.
My devotee, by understanding this,
Can take a step toward my state of being.   {19}

Know that Sentience and Substance
Are both beginningless as well.
Know that the adaptations, and the gunas,
Come to be in Substance.   {20}

It's said the work, the tool, and the worker
Have their cause in Substance.
It's said that Sentience is the reason
Pain and pleasure are experienced.   {21}

Sentience, in Substance stationed,
Enjoys the gunas born of nature.
Attachment to the gunas causes
Births in good or evil wombs.   {22}

Inside the body, the Highest Spirit
Is called the witness, buttress,
Authorizer, enjoyer,
Great Lord and highest atman.   {23}

Knowing Sentience and Substance this way,
Together with the gunas,
No matter how a man may live
He will not be reborn.   {24}

Some by meditation, others
By Samkhya yoga, others
Still by active yoga see
The atman, in the atman, by the atman.   {25}

Some, not knowing this, may hear
From others how to worship. Holding
What they hear to be their highest goal,
They, too, transcend their deaths.   {26}

Bull of the Bharatas, know this:
Whatever takes birth, moving
Or rooted, takes birth from the Field
Uniting with the Knower of the Field.   {27}

In all the species stands
The one same highest Lord
Who, when they perish, does not perish.
Whoever sees this, *sees*.   {28}

Seeing the one same Lord
Established everywhere,
He does his atman no self-harm.
From there he goes along the highest path.   {29}

Substance alone
Does every kind of doing.
Whoever sees this—that the atman
Is not the doer—*sees*.   {30}

When he sees that being's
Multiplicity stays all one
And then expands from there,
He will attain Brahman.   {31}

No beginning to it. No gunas.
This imperishable highest atman,
Arjuna, seated in the body
Does not act and is not smeared.   {32}

Just as the ether, pervasive
And subtle, can't be smeared,
The atman that sits in every
Body can't be smeared.   {33}

As the one sun, Arjuna,
Brightens the whole world,
The owner of the Field
Brightens the whole Field.   {34}

A knowing eye distinguishes
Between the Field and Knower of the Field.
Whoever knows how beings can be freed
From Substance goes on to the zenith.   {35}

Tell Apart the Three Gunas

Krishna describes the three gunas, Purity, Power, and Darkness. Everyone possesses all three to varying degrees; usually one predominates over the other two, and Krishna describes how each one manifests. Each individual perceives his or her predominant guna, and its manifestations, as the good. The ultimate good, according to Krishna, is to transcend the three gunas entirely.

Arjuna wonders how such a transcendent person behaves, and how he pulls off that transcendence in the first place. Krishna describes the detachment and equanimity familiar from earlier descriptions of the yogi.

The Blessed Lord said,

> The highest knowledge, best of all
> The kinds of knowledge, I'll proclaim again.
> All sages, knowing it, have gone
> From here to the highest perfection. {1}

> Come creation they do not take birth
> And come the dissolution do not tremble,
> Taking refuge in this knowledge,
> Coming to identify with me. {2}

> My womb is great Brahman.
> In this, I set the egg.
> The genesis of all species, Bharata,
> Engenders out of that. {3}

> As for the forms engendered
> In all wombs, son of Kunti,
> Brahman is their greater womb.
> I am the father, generous with seed. {4}

> Purity, Power, and Darkness:
> The gunas nature has engendered
> Bind down in the body
> Eternity's embodiment. {5}

> Purity—spotless, shining,
> Clear of sickness—binds it by
> Attaching it to happiness,
> Attaching it to knowledge. {6}

> Know that Power's very self is
> Passion born of thirst and clinging.
> This can bind the embodied atman
> By attaching it to action. {7}

Know that Darkness, born of ignorance,
Deluding every body
Binds this with distraction,
Laziness, and sleep.   {8}

Purity latches on to happiness
As Power does to action, Arjuna.
Obscuring knowledge, Darkness
Latches on to distractions.   {9}

Purity comes up by overcoming
Power and Darkness; Power,
By overcoming Purity and Darkness; Darkness,
By overcoming Purity and Power.   {10}

When this body's every gate
Lights up with knowledge,
You will know for sure that
Purity has burgeoned.   {11}

Greed, activity, starting
Projects, restlessness, desire:
Bull of the Bharatas, these spring up
When Power burgeons.   {12}

Dullness and inertia,
Distractibility, delusion:
These arise when Darkness
Burgeons, Arjuna.   {13}

When an embodied atman, grown great
In Purity, goes on to dissolution,
He sets foot on the stainless worlds
Of those who know the Highest.   {14}

When a Power-seeker goes to dissolution,
He is born with those attached to action.
Likewise, someone who dissolves in Darkness
Takes birth in deluded wombs. {15}

They say that work well done
Will bear a Pure and spotless fruit.
Of Power, though, the fruit is pain.
Ignorance is the fruit of Darkness. {16}

Purity gives birth to knowledge;
Power, to greed. Distractions,
Delusions, ignorance
Arise from Darkness. {17}

Upward go the Pure. The Power-
Seekers, in the middle, stay there.
Stuck in the basest guna,
The Dark must go below. {18}

When an observer sees
Nothing at work but gunas,
He knows what's higher than the gunas,
And so he comes to be me. {19}

Going beyond these three gunas
Born in the body, the one embodied—
Freed from birth and death, old age
And pain—can get to immortality. {20}

Arjuna said,
Someone who's gone beyond these
Three gunas, Lord—what marks him out?
What's his behavior? And how does he
Go beyond these three gunas? {21}

The Blessed Lord said,

Enlightenment, activity,
Delusion, Arjuna:
He does not scorn their presence.
He does not yearn for their absence. {22}

Seated apart, as if indifferent,
Unmoved by gunas, thinking,
"These are just the gunas in a whirl,"
He doesn't waver. He stands fast. {23}

Pleasure and pain the same thing, self-reliant,
A clod, a rock, and gold the same, steadfast,
Equal toward likes and dislikes,
Equal toward blame or praise, {24}

In honor or dishonor equal, equal
To the friendly faction or the hostile,
Renouncing all endeavors: He
Is said to go beyond the gunas. {25}

Whoever in the unswerving yoga
Of devotion serves me,
Going beyond these gunas: He
Is fit to become Brahman. {26}

I am the basis of Brahman,
Of immortality, of eternity,
Of the dharma's perpetuation
And of the blissful singularity. {27}

The Highest Human Godhood

Krishna begins with the complex metaphor of an upside-down tree. By scaling that metaphorical tree—by getting to the root of existence—you get to a place from which there is no return to suffering and rebirth.

Krishna expands on the idea of how every life is an embodiment of something divine. It takes a striving yogi to perceive that.

To show how the divine is both without and within, Krishna locates himself in the earth, providing food, and in the stomach, digesting food. He is the "Highest Human Godhood" because he transcends the ephemeral and the permanent alike.

The Blessed Lord said,

Roots on high and boughs below,
The imperishable asvattha tree
Has hymns for leaves. They say
Whoever knows it knows the Vedas.   {1}

Below and above it spreads its boughs,
Nourished by gunas, sprouting what we sense.
Its roots stretch out below, entangling
Actions in the human world.   {2}

Here in the world, the form of it can't be perceived,
Not its end, not its beginning, not its foundation.
Cutting, with detachment's hard weapon,
This asvattha tree's well-planted root,   {3}

You must pursue a path to the place
Where those who go do not return again.
I seek refuge in that primal spirit
Energy flowed out of long ago.   {4}

No pride and no delusion, guilty attachments conquered,
Forever in the metaself, desires turned away,
Freed from the opposites known as joy and sorrow,
They go, undeluded, to that imperishable place.   {5}

The sun does not illumine,
Nor the rabbit moon, nor fire,
That highest home of mine
Where those who go do not return.   {6}

Just a fragment of me in the living
World becomes a life, eternal,
And draws the senses (six, including
Mind) that rest in nature.   {7}

When the Lord takes on a body
And also when he leaves it, these
Are what he takes along with him
As a wind does perfumes from their source.   {8}

Presiding over hearing, vision,
Touch and taste and smell
As well as mind,
This savors what it senses.   {9}

Whether he steps out of it, or stays in,
Or enjoys the body with the gunas,
Deluded people do not see him.
The eye of knowledge sees him.   {10}

Striving yogis see him
Stationed in the atman; thoughtless,
Unperfected atmans, even
When they strive to, do not see him.   {11}

The brilliance coming from the sun
That makes the whole world shine,
That brilliance in the moon
And fire: Know it to be mine.   {12}

Entering the ground, I support
Species with my vigor.
Becoming Soma, soul of flavor,
I flourish all my herbs.   {13}

Becoming metabolic fire,
I shelter in the breathing body,
Yoked to breathing in and breathing out,
And I digest four kinds of food.   {14}

I am seated in the hearts of everyone.
From me come memory, knowledge, and forgetting,
And I alone am what all the Vedas know.
Crafter of Vedanta, knower of the Vedas: me. {15}

The perishable and imperishable
Are spirits twinned within the world.
The perishable one is in all creatures.
What stands upon the peak is called imperishable. {16}

Still, the *highest* spirit is another,
Named the Highest Self,
Who enters and bears up the three worlds,
Their eternal Lord. {17}

Going as I do beyond the perishable,
Higher even than the imperishable,
I am celebrated as the Highest Human Godhood
In the world and in the Vedas. {18}

Someone who without delusion
Knows me as the Highest Human Godhood
Knows it all and worships me
With all his being, Arjuna. {19}

And so I've spoken this most
Secret precept, sinless one.
Awakening to it will make you wise,
And what needs doing will be done. {20}

Tell the Divine from the Demonic Inheritance

Krishna details two kinds of human inheritance, the divine and the demonic. After assuring Arjuna that he has a divine inheritance, Krishna dwells at length on the demonic one. The punishment of such people after death takes the form of rebirth in a demonic womb, and so the cycle perpetuates itself.

Krishna exhorts Arjuna to renounce lust, rage, and greed, and to let the scripture guide him in the work he must do here, on earth.

The Blessed Lord said,

Fearlessness, purity of heart,
Staying yoked through knowledge,
Charity, self-control, and sacrifice,
Study, austerity, simplicity;   {1}

Ahimsa, truth, renunciation,
Kindness, creaturely compassion,
Serenity, and modesty;
No rage, no lust, no fickleness, no slander;   {2}

Brilliance, patience, courage, cleanliness,
No treachery and no vainglory:
These traits belong to someone, Bharata,
Born with a divine inheritance.   {3}

Fraudulence, arrogance, narcissism,
Anger, coarseness, ignorance
Belong to someone, Partha,
Born with a demonic inheritance.   {4}

Inheritance can free you, if divine,
But if demonic, it can bind you.
Don't grieve: Your divinity's inherent.
You were born a son of Pandu.   {5}

Two kinds of beings are created
In this world, demonic and divine.
Divine ones I've extensively explained—
On the demonic, Partha, hear me out.   {6}

Demonic people don't know
What to do, what not to do,
Or purity, or proper conduct.
No finding any truth in them!   {7}

"No truth, no base," they say, "no lord
Is in the world. It came to be,
But one thing doesn't follow from another.
What else causes it but lust?"   {8}

Holding to this view,
Lost souls with small minds
Emerge as enemies, cruel
In action, to destroy the world.   {9}

Harboring a lust that's hard to fill,
Showy and arrogant and drunk,
Deluded, grasping after false ideas,
They proceed with dirty purposes.   {10}

Obsessing over countless worries
They die with in the end,
Enjoying lust, their highest aim—
Concerning *that,* they're all conviction—   {11}

Trapped and roped by a hundred hopes,
Devout in lust and rage,
Intending to enjoy their lusts, they strive
To stockpile wealth illegally.   {12}

"This is how much I profited today,
And this, the chariot I have in mind,
And this, and this as well, is mine,
And more wealth in the future!   {13}

I killed that enemy,
And I'll kill others, too!
I am the Lord! I am the enjoyer!
I am perfect, strong, and happy!   {14}

How rich I am, how well-born!
Who else is like me?
I'll sacrifice, I'll donate, I'll rejoice!"
So they say, by ignorance deluded. {15}

With many fancies leading them astray,
In a net of delusion entangled,
Attached to lust's enjoyment,
They fall into an unclean hell. {16}

Self-absorbed and stubborn,
Full of wealth and pride and drunkenness,
Their sacrifice, though called a sacrifice,
Is mere hypocrisy without the rite rules. {17}

They cling to egotism, force,
Insolence, lust, and anger.
In every body, their own or someone else's,
It's *me* their envy hates. {18}

These hateful sadists, mankind's
Basest, I am always hurling
Into cycles of rebirth
In hexed demonic wombs. {19}

Entering demonic wombs
Birth after birth, deluded people
Don't attain me, son of Kunti.
From there they take the lowest path. {20}

Through Lust and Rage and Greed,
This triple gate of Hell,
The atman perishes. That's why
You should renounce this triad. {21}

Arjuna, getting free of these
Three dark gates, a man
Has done the best thing for himself.
From there he takes the highest path.   {22}

Whoever throws out scripture's rules
And turns where his desire makes him
Does not attain perfection,
Happiness, or the highest path.   {23}

So let the scripture be your standard
And settle what to do, what not to do.
Knowing what the rule of scripture says,
You should do your work—*here*.   {24}

Tell Apart the Three Kinds of Faith

Arjuna asks whether someone who throws out strict scriptural rules is in a state of Purity, Power, or Darkness.

Krishna details how the three gunas influence the religious aspects of life. The three gunas structure Krishna's classifications of faith, diet, sacrifices, austerities, and charity.

He finishes with a description of the mantra *Aum Tat Sat*.

Arjuna said,

Worshippers who throw out
Scripture's rules, though full of faith—
What is their condition, Krishna?
Purity, Power, or Darkness?   {1}

The Blessed Lord said,

Faith can be of three kinds, each one
Born of an embodied being's
Own nature: Pure, Power-crazed,
And Dark. Now hear of this.   {2}

Truth takes on the shape of
Each man's faith, Arjuna.
Man is made of faith.
As his faith is, he is.   {3}

Purity worships Gods, while Power
Worships Rakshasas and Yakshas.
Others, in the Darkness, worship
Ghosts and crowds of spirits.   {4}

Men who sear themselves with awful
Austerities that scriptures don't ordain—
Yoked to showiness and egotism,
To lust and force and passion—   {5}

Harrow thoughtlessly
The body's vital organs.
It is *me* they harrow in their bodies.
Know them for determined demons.   {6}

Even the foods that people like divide
In three, as do their sacrifices,
Austerities, and gifts.
Hear out these distinctions.   {7}

Longevity, virtue, strength, health,
Happiness, satisfaction: Foods that
Promote these, juicy, hearty, smooth,
And firm, are foods the Pure prefer. {8}

Pungent, sour, salty, scorchingly
Hot and harsh and spicy: Such are
Foods that Power-seekers wish for,
Causing pain, disease, and sorrow. {9}

Spoiled, flavorless,
Putrid leftovers,
Unclean refuse: That's
The fodder Darkness likes. {10}

Sacrifice offered up observantly
Without expecting its fruition
By a mind that concentrates on
Offering the right thing: That is Pure. {11}

But when it has the fruit in view
And offers with the aim of showing off—
Best of the Bharatas, beware,
That sacrifice is after Power. {12}

Stripped of rules, no offerings of rice,
Stripped of mantras, no donations:
Sacrifice that's destitute
Of faith is seen as Dark. {13}

Worshipping Gods, the twice-born, gurus,
And wise men; cleanliness, uprightness,
Chastity, ahimsa: These
Are called the bodily austerities. {14}

Words that cause no worry,
Truthful, pleasing, helpful,
Studied recitations to yourself:
These are called austerities of speech. {15}

Serenity of mind, gentleness,
Silence, self-restraint,
Purification of emotions:
These are called austerities of mind. {16}

Yoked, without expecting
Its fruition, men of utmost faith
Burn with this threefold austerity,
And it is seen as Pure. {17}

Austerity that's done for show
Or for the sake of getting favors, honors,
Reverence: Here we call that
Power-crazed and fleeting, fickle. {18}

Austerity that's done as torture
With a muddled grasp of atman
Or for the sake of someone's ruin—
That's described as Dark. {19}

A gift for the sake of giftgiving
Given to return no favor, to a worthy
Person at the proper place and time:
That gift will be recalled as Pure. {20}

A grudging gift that's given
For the sake of getting favors
Back or aiming for results—that gift
Will be recalled as Power-seeking. {21}

A gift without a sense of place and timing
Given to unworthy people
Disrespectfully or in contempt:
That is declared to be Dark.   {22}

Aum Tat Sat is Brahman's
Threefold mnemonic gloss.
By this, the Brahmins, Vedas,
And sacrifices were ordained of old.   {23}

That's why declaring *Aum* is always
How Brahman's interpreters
Preface, as the precepts tell them,
Sacrifices, gifts, austerities.   {24}

Tat say those who yearn for freedom,
Doing varied acts of sacrifice,
Austerity, and giving,
Never aiming at their fruit.   {25}

Meaning "good," or meaning "real"—
That's how *Sat* is used.
For worthy work, too, Partha,
The syllable *Sat* is used.   {26}

Sat, they say, is staying steadfast
In sacrifice, austerity, and giving,
And any action with that purpose
Gets the designation *Sat*.   {27}

To pour an offering or undertake
Austerity without the faith
Is called *Asat*—and it is nothing to us,
Partha. Not here, not hereafter.   {28}

Free Yourself Through Renunciation

Arjuna asks to know the difference between the two kinds of estrangement from worldly life: relinquishment and renunciation.

Krishna defines relinquishment as giving up the fruits of action, and he uses the gunas to classify it three ways. Agency itself, according to Krishna, has five different components. Because the atman is not one of these, a soldier like Arjuna, "even when he kills these people / Doesn't kill."

The gunas structure Krishna's threefold classifications of several things: knowledge, work, will, resolve, intellect, and happiness. The gunas also guide the natural duties of different kinds of people—in Arjuna's case, a warrior's duties. That work, even if it's done imperfectly, is still important and necessary.

Krishna describes again the ideal yogi, the one who knows him and becomes Brahman. He exhorts Arjuna to take refuge in him, insisting that Arjuna is going to fight this war anyway, even against his will.

For a moment he seems to finish, telling Arjuna to do what he wants to do—but then he keeps going to tell his friend he loves him. After all his teachings and visions, this love is "the secret of all secrets."

Between the armies on Kurukshetra, Arjuna stands up again and resolves to fight.

Back in the throne room of King Dhritarashtra, Sanjaya speaks of his joy at overhearing this conversation. His last words assert the righteous splendor—and triumph—of Krishna and Arjuna.

Arjuna said,
> Renunciation of the world, Krishna:
> I want to know the truth
> That separates this from
> Relinquishment of the world.   {1}

The Blessed Lord said,
> As poets see it, renunciation
> Casts aside the act of craving.
> The clear-eyed see relinquishment
> As giving up the fruits of action.   {2}

> Some wise men say, "Relinquish
> All action," since it's sinful. Others say
> Sacrifice, austerity, and giving
> Are actions not to be relinquished.   {3}

> Arjuna, you tiger of a man,
> Hear out my conviction on
> Relinquishment. Relinquishment
> Is classified three ways.   {4}

> Sacrifice, austerity, and giving
> Are works far better done than given up.
> Sacrifice, austerity, and giving
> Purify the mindful.   {5}

> These works, though, ought to be performed
> Relinquishing attachment to their fruits.
> This, Arjuna, without a doubt
> Is my utmost belief.   {6}

> It isn't proper to renounce
> The work demanded of you.
> It's said that such deluded
> Relinquishment is Dark.   {7}

When someone gives up work because it's hard,
Or else from fear he'll hurt his body—that's
His Power guna, giving up. Of such
"Relinquishment" he'll never gain the fruit.   {8}

Dutifully doing work
Because it is demanded of you,
Attachment to its fruit relinquished—
That relinquishment is Pure.   {9}

Not hating an unpleasant action,
To pleasant action unattached,
The man of wisdom, cut free from doubt,
Gives action up and fills with truth.   {10}

No one borne inside a body
Can relinquish actions altogether,
So call someone who gives up action's fruit
A man of true relinquishment.   {11}

Wanted, unwanted, mixed:
For those who give up nothing as they die,
Action bears three kinds of fruit.
Renouncing it bears none at all.   {12}

Five factors—so the Samkhya
Doctrine has concluded—
Execute all actions.
Learn these from me, Arjuna: {13}

The bodily abode, the will,
Means of many kinds,
Many kinds of motion.
The God among these is the fifth.   {14}

Whatever act a man initiates
With body, mind, or language,
Either righteous or perverse,
These five originate it,   {15}

And that's the truth. Whoever looks
With an imperfect intellect will see
The doer as himself alone.
His thick skull doesn't see at all.   {16}

A man who isn't egocentric,
His intelligence unsullied,
Even when he kills these people
Doesn't kill and isn't bound.   {17}

Knowledge, the known, the knower
Are action's triple impetus.
The means, the work, the worker
Are action's three components.   {18}

Samkhya's guna theory
Distinguishes three kinds
Of knowledge, work, and worker.
It's only right you hear of these, too.   {19}

To see, in all these species, one
Imperishable Being,
Diverse but indivisible:
Know that knowledge to be Pure.   {20}

The knowledge that knows all
These species one by one
As manifold and many: Know
That knowledge to be after Power.   {21}

To cling to one slight thing
As if it's all there is,
No cause, no real purpose:
That knowledge, I declare, is Dark.   {22}

Detached, deliberate work
That's done with no desire, no hate,
No wish to get its fruits—
I say that work is Pure.   {23}

Work that's done to get some wish,
Self-seekingly, or else
You overwork yourself to do it:
I say that will is after Power.   {24}

No thought of upshot, damage, harm,
Much less your own ability—
I say that any such confused
Initiative is in the Dark.   {25}

Freed from attachments, never talking
Yourself up, full of grit and zest,
Undisturbed in failure or success:
I say that will is Pure.   {26}

Hectic for the fruit of action,
Dirty, greedy, savage,
Now sorrowful, now joyful: I
Declare that will is after Power.   {27}

Unyoked and vulgar, stubborn,
Wicked, lying, lazy,
Depressed, procrastinating:
I say that will is in the Dark.   {28}

The gunas split in three
Resolve and intellect.
Arjuna, hear me set them out
Distinctly and in full.   {29}

Extroversion, introversion,
Taboo and duty, threat and nonthreat,
Bondage and freedom—knowing these,
An intellect is Pure.   {30}

Dharma or adharma, Partha,
Duty or taboo—a Power-
Seeking intellect will make
Mistakes distinguishing the two.   {31}

But when it thinks adharma *is*
Its dharma, Partha, darkly
Enveloped, everything inverted,
An intellect is in the Dark.   {32}

Resolve that resolutely holds
The mind, the breath, the senses
In unswerving yoga:
Arjuna, that resolve is Pure.   {33}

But when, attached and hoping
For the fruit, resolve resolves
On wishes, riches, and roles it plays,
Arjuna, that resolve is Power-crazed.   {34}

Sleepiness, terror, sorrow,
Vanity, depression: When
A dimwit just will not renounce these,
Arjuna, his resolve is Dark.   {35}

Now hear about the threefold
Happiness, Bull of the Bharatas.
Studying how to enjoy it,
You reach the end of suffering. {36}

What starts out as a poison, then
Evolves into something ambrosial: I
Proclaim that happiness is Pure,
A bright gift born of your own mind. {37}

What starts out like ambrosia
Where the senses touch it, then
Evolves into a poison—such,
I say, is Power's happiness. {38}

A happiness from start to finish
Self-deceiving, risen out
Of sleep and sloth and apathy:
I say that happiness is Dark. {39}

No being born of nature,
On earth or yet in heaven
Among the Gods, is free
Of these three gunas. {40}

According to the gunas
Arising from their inborn nature,
Brahmins, soldiers, peasants,
And sudras share out work. {41}

Calm, restraint, austerity;
Cleanliness, patience, honesty;
Knowledge, judgment, faith:
This is the work innate to Brahmins. {42}

Bravery, brilliance, staunchness, skill,
Never running from a battle,
Charity, authority:
This is the work innate to warriors.   {43}

Plowing, care of cattle, commerce:
This is the work innate to peasants.
Doing acts of service:
This is the work innate to sudras.   {44}

Each man pleased in his own work,
Each man gains fulfillment.
How can someone find fulfillment
In his own work? Hear me out: {45}

Worshipping through his own work
The origin of beings,
The one pervading all this,
A man can find fulfillment.   {46}

Better your own dharma botched
Than someone else's dharma done well.
Working as your nature dictates,
You will not take on sin.   {47}

You shouldn't give up work
That you were born to, even if
It's flawed. Fault envelops all
Endeavors, as smoke does fire.   {48}

Intellect on all sides unattached,
Self overcome and longing gone,
Renunciation gets him to
The stasis of supreme perfection.   {49}

Perfection once attained, the highest
State of knowledge is Brahman.
Briefly, Arjuna, learn from me
How you can gain that, too. {50}

Sensual things relinquished, words first,
Intellect cleansed and yoked,
Resolved on self-reserve,
Rejecting hate and passion, {51}

Living alone and eating light,
Controlled in body, talk, and thought,
Constantly exalted in his yogic focus,
Neutrality his refuge; {52}

Egoism, brute force, pride,
Lust, rage, possessiveness
Abandoned; selfless, calm:
He has evolved to become Brahman. {53}

Once it has become Brahman, the atman
Does not mourn and does not yearn. At peace,
The same toward and in all beings,
He gains the height of my devotion. {54}

By devotion to me, he comes to know
Just how and who I really am,
And once he knows the real me
He enters me immediately. {55}

Always doing all his works
With me his sanctuary,
By my grace he gains
A home eternal, deathless. {56}

Surrendering in mind all works
To me, with me your highest object,
Take refuge in an intellectual yoga.
Always think of me.   {57}

Think of me, and by my grace
You'll get through all kinds of hard going.
But if your ego will not listen,
You are going to be destroyed.   {58}

If you shelter in your egoism,
Thinking to yourself, "I will not fight,"
This resolve of yours will be in vain.
Your nature will command you.   {59}

Bound by your own karma,
Born to your own nature,
What you in your confusion do not want
To do, you *will* do. Even against your will.   {60}

The Lord of all creatures
Lives in the homeland heart.
It whirls all the creatures
Maya ties to the machine.   {61}

Go with all your being,
Arjuna, and shelter in him.
By *his* grace you will gain
The highest peace, the perpetual home.   {62}

I've explained to you a knowledge
More secret than the Secret.
Mull this over, the whole of it.
Do what you want to do. . . .   {63}

Hear me out again. My highest word,
The secret of all secrets:
I love you. Hard. That's why
I speak, to do you good. {64}

Mind on me, to me devote yourself,
Sacrifice for me, to me make reverence,
And it's to *me* that you will come—
I promise you—because you're dear to me. {65}

Relinquish all your dharmas.
Come shelter in me,
And I will free you
From all sins. Never grieve. {66}

Don't speak of this to anyone
Who lacks for rigor, shirks devotion,
Or doesn't care to hear what's said,
Nor to anyone who envies me. {67}

Whoever glosses this, the highest
Secret, for my devotees
Enacts the highest devotion to me,
And he will come to me without a doubt. {68}

No one in all mankind
Will do a thing to please me more.
No one on earth will be
Dearer to me than he is. {69}

And anyone who studies this
Dharmic dialogue of ours
Through the knowledge sacrifice
Loves me: This is my belief. {70}

Even if a man just hears it,
Full of faith and never scoffing,
He, too, will gain his freedom,
The work of virtue, its joyful worlds.   {71}

Have you heard this, Partha,
Single-mindedly?
Has your unknowing,
Your delusion, perished?   {72}

Arjuna said,
My delusion has perished. My memory gains.
By your grace, ever-enduring one,
I stand here now. My doubts are gone.
I will do what you command.   {73}

Sanjaya said,
I have heard this conversation
Between that great soul Arjuna
And Krishna. It's so wondrous
It makes my hair stand on end.   {74}

By Vyasa's grace, I heard
This highest, secret yoga
From the Lord of yoga. Krishna
Himself related it, before my eyes!   {75}

King, I recall and recall
This holy, wondrous conversation
Of Arjuna and Krishna,
And again and again I rejoice.   {76}

I recall and recall that
Beyond-wondrous form of God,
And great is my amazement, King,
And once more, and once more, I rejoice.   {77}

Wherever Krishna Lord of yoga is,
Wherever Arjuna the archer is,
There must be splendor, triumph, wealth,
And ethics. This is my belief.   {78}

Listener's Guides

The Gita opens in a palace deserted except for two men: an elderly king, Dhritarashtra, sitting forward nervously on his throne, and his preternaturally calm advisor, Sanjaya. Something is wrong with both men's eyes. The King is blind, and he blinks rapidly but blankly at the floor. Sanjaya's eyes focus ahead of him, into the distance.

This is a palace that has known the clamor of a hundred rowdy sons, but the King's sons, the Kauravas, are all gone now, mustered with their allies for battle on a far-off plain. They are fighting a civil war against their cousins.

The King is desperate for news from the front. Luckily for the blind King, Sanjaya possesses eyesight mystically keen. Long before any messenger can gallop the distance, Sanjaya can give an eyewitness report of everything happening on Kurukshetra. He stares through eyes cataract-grayblue toward a faraway battlefield. He sees a hot, dusty plain in North India on which two armies have lined up, facing each other.

His gaze projects the figures on the throne room floor: a haughty-looking, handsome young prince, Duryodhan, stands next to an elderly man, Drona. Drona wears, under his armor, diagonally across his chest, the white thread of the priesthood, his original calling.

Duryodhan is Dhritarashtra's eldest son. With his fists on his hips, he surveys the Pandava Army.

Sanjaya's lips murmur like a sleeptalker's. No wonder the first word he says is *seeing*.

A voice impossibly deep erupts out of Sanjaya's throat. It isn't his; it belongs to Duryodhan. Sanjaya has drifted up onto his feet in the blind King's throne room. Now, inhabiting his role, inhabited by his role, he starts strutting back and forth, pointing out warrior after opposing warrior, just as Duryodhan is doing, hundreds of miles away.

❧

Duryodhan's verses, as reported by Sanjaya, are the least philosophical ones in the Gita, and with good reason. The blind King's eldest son is a character familiar from classical literature—he resembles a chest-thumping Homeric brute like Agamemnon, or the *miles gloriosus* (braggart soldier) of ancient Latin literature.

So immediately after admiring the Pandava Army, Duryodhan falls back on bragging. He brags to his own elderly instructor in the arts of war, the "twice-born" Brahmin Drona. One imagines the young prince does this out of stung pride, and also out of creeping fear.

This fear explains his shout, at the end, to all his officers to guard Bhishma. Bhishma is not just one of the most powerful warriors on the battlefield. He is also, by far, the oldest, wearing a gray beard for a second breastplate. The civil war is not just between two sets of cousins; it is multigenerational, having drawn in a relative of their grandfather's generation.

❧

A major division in the poem is marked by the sounding of the conch shells. To my mind, it signals the transition from the framing *Mahabharata* epic to the stand-alone philosophical poem we know as the Gita.

Accordingly, Sanjaya and Dhritarashtra are only implicit presences from this point onward. All that is left of them is their absence—and Sanjaya's voice. With Sanjaya as our guide, our focus flies to the opposite end of the field, to the Pandava Army, quiet until this moment.

A chariot detaches from the formation and heads for the no-man's-land between the two armies.

That chariot holds Krishna and Arjuna. Both princes come of illustrious ancestry, and Sanjaya refers to that in his epithets for them. He is placing them in the context of their families, Arjuna in particular. After all, Kurukshetra is about to witness an intrafamilial war. Family considerations trigger the tragic aria that forms the climax of this introductory chapter—and best expresses its theme: "Arjuna Despairs."

❧

Such subtitles, by the way, are found in every edition of the Gita, and I have included them here. I thought about not doing so: They were appended to the text by the theologian Adi Shankara (ninth century C.E.), possibly a millennium into the Gita's history. The Gita's original listeners, including Arjuna himself, did not have them.

At this point, though, they have been part of the Gita for longer than they haven't. So I have kept them as headings for the capsule summaries on the title pages of the sessions.

Why *session*? Other English translations label each section of the Gita a "book," "chapter," or "discourse." The Sanskrit word is *adhyaya,* which also has the meaning of "lesson" or "lecture." Yet the image those words conjure—of a professor giving a student lesson after lesson, lecture after lecture—is a bit wrong for the Gita.

The Gita is a conversation between friends. It is also a polyphonic song. After all, it's not like Sanjaya's narration and Arjuna's questions are in prose, while Krishna alone gets the poetry. The Gita, to borrow a term from the parlance of music drama, is "sung-through."

In English, *session* has a place in music parlance. A "music session" or "jam session" implies collective, informal, spontaneous creativity. It fits the Gita better. Etymologically, too, the word *session* comes from the Latin for "sitting." Adi Shankara was also the first to classify the Gita as the last Upanishad. The word *Upanishad* derives, in part, from the Sanskrit word for "sitting."

Because the subtitles are ones a theologian made up rather than words of the Gita itself, I allowed myself a little freedom in their translation. The Sanskrit titles contain the word *yoga* after every phrase. Even the first session is literally the "Arjuna-Despair-Yoga." Following Shankara's formula in English would elide how the Gita is not just a didactic poem but an imperative one. Yoga, whether the modern physical version or the ancient existential one, is something you learn by doing. I translated the purely descriptive titles into purely descriptive titles and the rest into forms that are at once descriptive and imperative. So "Bhakti Yoga" becomes not "The Yoga of Devotion" but "Devote Yourself."

The first session of the Gita has bits and flourishes that resemble a heroic epic—the residuum of the *Mahabharata*. Starting with this first question from Arjuna, the Gita takes on the traits of another peak of Hindu scripture—the middle Himalaya, between the Vedas and the Gita, known collectively as the Upanishads.

The Upanishads are frequently question-and-answer sessions between a guru and a pupil. Inquiry is central to their structure and spirit. Kena Upanishad, for example, means, literally, "The From-What-Cause? Upanishad," and Prasna Upanishad means "The Question Upanishad."

Arjuna, at this point, is merely asking a question of his friend and counselor. He does not know he is speaking to an avatar of Vishnu. Even after he finds out, in Session 11, he *still* keeps asking questions. This boldness—and the highest possible Authority's openness to being questioned—is not new in the tradition of the Upanishads. In Katha Upanishad, for example, a fearless boy named Nachiketa heads down to interrogate Yama, the God of Death, about the nature of life.

So the Gita switches its model here, moving from the heroic epic to the dialogue. The dialogue will concern theology and philosophy. It will encompass what we would today call psychology and ethics as well.

In the Indian tradition, theology and philosophy are not so distinct as they are in the West's part-pagan, part-Judeo-Christian tradition. Imagine if the work of thought between Aristotle and Aquinas were unbroken by any continent-wide conversion. Our even later division of thought into university departments is still more alien to the Gita's world, just as it was to that of Aristotle—who lectured in the morning about *Nicomachean Ethics,* in the early afternoon about *Metaphysics,* in the late afternoon on *Politics,* and finished with an evening session *On Youth, Old Age, Life and Death, and Respiration.* Krishna, too, covers all those subjects, and then some.

～

Just as the Gita shifts its nature in this session, so does Krishna—and more than once. From the obedient charioteer of Session 1 he turns, at first, into a brother-in-arms, shaming Arjuna into action.

Our narrator, Sanjaya, is right to notice the laughter of Krishna at the moment of that first transition. He is making light of Arjuna's despair. This trivialization is also present when Krishna calls the dead and the living *gatasun* and *agatasun,* people whose breath has gone out of them and people whose breath hasn't. As if dead bodies are just balloons that happen to have deflated. This way of saying it trivializes death in order to trivialize killing—which is exactly what Krishna, the counselor, wants to do for his despondent warrior right now: show the task from a perspective that will make it less horrific.

Yet his laughter vanishes almost immediately. Krishna follows this perspective out, out, until he has zoomed out to the most detached vantage point possible, and the cold eye of the soldier becomes the cold eye of eternity. The despair seems a minor thing, and so does the war itself. That hectoring, drill sergeant's tone was just Krishna testing out an approach. After working the shame angle a bit, Krishna shifts personae again, this time to a sublime religious philosopher.

In this role, he speaks of Samkhya, one of the oldest traditional schools of philosophy. He speaks of yoga, using the word in its broadest sense, as a many-faceted spiritual practice, with its roots in "joining" and "yoking." And inevitably—how could he not?—he speaks of karma, the cycle of action and consequence, the very thing Arjuna fears most.

With his new, philosophical tone, Krishna refers to "this." By "this," he doesn't mean Arjuna's body, the more present, visible external self. Instead he means "this" embodied atman. Grammatically, he refers to the inapparent part of Arjuna as the nearer of two things—not that, there, but *this*, here.

It is a well-known division: You are not your body, you are what your body embodies. Krishna says more about the atman, beginning with a metaphor that, ingeniously, uses the body as a stand-in for the atman.

At one point, Krishna lays into the shiftless, shallow wisdom of the irresolute—but the example he gives isn't the expected one, that of people with short attention spans, who are trend-obsessed and frenetic. Instead, he depicts a specific religious type: rigid, narrow-minded, ritual-bound—and, under the holy exterior, utterly worldly.

ت

Until now, these conversations have been best friend to best friend, prince to prince, and, since the war began, archer to charioteer. For years before this war, Krishna served as a strategist and diplomat on behalf of Arjuna and the Pandava brothers. Arjuna has only rarely seen Krishna grow openly philosophical like this.

The shift inverts the usual relationship between archer and charioteer, the one calling out where and when to turn, the other steering the horses. Now the archer subordinates himself to his charioteer's direction. Arjuna takes the opportunity, this glimpse of a hidden and private depth, to get more out of Krishna. His question has to do with how to behave—what the external signals of enlightenment are, in speech and deportment.

Arjuna refers to *stitha-prajna,* where *stitha* means,

roughly, "steady," and *prajna* is a word that comes from the root word for knowledge but has an intensifying prefix attached to it. This root word, *jna,* is shared with another Indo-European language, Greek, where it blossomed into *gnosis.* Gnosticism shares an uncanny, not-entirely-coincidental resemblance to Vedantic thought, but using "steady gnosis" and "steady gnostic" would muddy the linguistic waters.

I settled on "steady mystic" because the phrase is less specific to a different religious tradition. It focuses on the subject of that "intensified" knowing—the mystical understanding of the many being the One. Every mystical tradition that bears the name, from Mansur al-Hallaj's Sufi *fana'a* to Meister Eckhart's Christian *unio mystica,* has arrived at this numerical conclusion, like independent geometers around the globe deriving the same value for pi. In other words, I substitute for the word that refers to the most intense knowing (Sanskrit, *prajna*) the word that refers to the most intense secret (Greek, *mystikos*).

❧

Krishna, in the course of his answer, hints at the larger transformation to come: from theologian to Theos. He drops this hint very casually, with no portentous change of form or size or appearance. It comes in a phrase that takes up very little space in Sanskrit—*mat param*—"with me his zenith," literally, "with me his highest [goal or object]." I resisted the urge to capitalize that "me." Arjuna's friend has just referred to himself as someone greater than a charioteer or prince or philosopher. The voice—the voice whose mouthpiece is the mouth of Krishna—has spoken up for the first time, no ventriloquy. It has referred to itself as what it is, divine.

❧

Notice that Arjuna's despair arises from a perversion of empathy and identification—a self-destructive, adharmic application of Vedantic teaching.

Vedanta, after all, encourages the seeker to empathize and identify with everything alive. It does so by teaching how your atman and all the other atmans in all the other species are identical (*identical* comes from the Latin word for "same"). You realize you are the same as they are because you realize we are all Brahman. This is a simple idea that is very hard to practice in real life, so hard it takes multiple births to do it right. It's hard not just because it's hard to perceive the spiritual sameness in a human being, an animal, and a plant. (How easy protecting the environment would be if that weren't the case!)

In Arjuna's case, this idea, incompletely understood, makes him vulnerable. Arjuna's empathy and identification exist, at this early stage in the Gita, without a balancing sense of dharma—his duty in the world, to the world.

Arjuna's despair originates when he identifies with *all* his extended family, including the relatives who want to kill him. He even prefers being killed by them to killing them. This is the *moha,* the delusion, that Krishna's wisdom will seek to correct. Krishna will do this through a variety of philosophical and psychological tactics—maybe *wisdoms* is the right word here.

Parked between the two armies, Arjuna identifies with the multiplicity before him. This is what weakens his will and makes him refuse to fight. Krishna's task will be to teach his friend how to differentiate between his own side and the opposing side—and how, for the sake of dharma, he must fight for one, and against the other.

ى

I can imagine an alternative, more contained Gita in which the last lines of Session 2 bring us close to the end of the whole interpolated episode. Arjuna has despaired; Krishna has given him a pep talk, first as a worldly warrior, then as an otherworldly thinker. Tack on the last segment of Session 18, and that's a fine episode.

Fortunately, episodes and interpolations in that longest of all epics, the *Mahabharata,* don't bother much with dramatic economy. The Gita creates its own nested frame of reference, its own sense of time, and unfolds at its leisure, according to its own poetic biorhythm. So Krishna and Arjuna actually have sixteen more sessions in which to talk things out.

Arjuna has his next question ready.

Arjuna sets off this session by making a reasonable enough objection. With all this exaltation of wisdom and knowing, whose ultimate goal is attaining extinction in Brahman, why do all this battlefield killing in the first place? Why not go off somewhere and meditate?

It's a question that had special relevance in the Hindu world. Most religious traditions have some sense of the active life and the contemplative life—the mission in the bad part of town, and the monastery on the mountaintop—but always to varying degrees. In Hindu India, the tendency to retreat from the world seems to have been particularly strong, helped along, perhaps, by the fourth and last stage of the idealized Hindu life, ascetic renunciation. The earliest known reference to Indian wise men in Western literature, in the *Histories* of Herodotus, refers to "Gymnosophists" who lived off in the forest, naked, and did what were probably yogic austerities. It's not that Krishna wants to discredit this choice. He just doesn't think it's the right one for a warrior like Arjuna on a battlefield like Kurukshetra.

The word that Arjuna uses twice in reference to the prospect of violence has the same root as *yoga*—"to yoke" or "to join." Krishna has spoken of yoking Arjuna's atman to Brahman, and Arjuna's life to the practice of yoga. Arjuna turns this around, speaking of someone (himself) "yoked" to a horrific action, "even if unwilling." Arjuna's use of the word comes from the agricultural source-image of yoga: that of a beast, yoked to the plow and goaded forward. His use of the word is a way of telling Krishna, implicitly: *You preach this exalted joining, but on this battlefield, what you're doing is enjoining me to butcher.*

So Krishna spends much of Session 3 encouraging Arjuna to act. Part of his argument involves drawing an equivalence between the divine and the human when it comes to activity. The move hinges on a double meaning in Sanskrit that fortuitously matches one in English: the way *loka* can mean both the planet itself and the people of the planet. When we say the "whole world is talking about" something, we are referring to people, while when we say "map of the world," we mean a map of the earth. (French does this, too, with *le monde*.)

Krishna compares what would happen if he, the God, stopped working. Krishna, of course, is also the Sustainer, Vishnu, and so he speaks of worlds dropping away and species dying out. But if Arjuna, as one of the best of men, doesn't do his work, something similar would happen to the world—that is, to society. Krishna makes a point of how important it is for someone as prominent as Prince Arjuna to set an example for the rest of his society.

The role the two sustainers have in common relates to *cohesion*. The cohesion of planets in orbit around the sun and the cohesion of matter itself, with electrons orbiting a nucleus, are the macrocosm and microcosm that Krishna sustains. He functions as invisibly as gravity. A great leader, like Arjuna, has a similar function in making people cohere in a society. Through dharmic action, he must "hold the world together." He need not be the center point, holding court, like a sun or a king or a nucleus. Arjuna, after all, is fighting to restore his eldest brother, not himself, to the throne. But he must work as the gravity that helps a society cohere.

That is the social role of the "best of men." Not retreat: engagement. He doesn't just go to work in the world. He encourages others to do so as well, attached to action though they are. Krishna explains the wise man's role in encouraging unwise people to do the right thing even as he encourages Arjuna to do the right thing. And so he continues the analogy between the divine and human, Brahman and atman, that scaffolds all of Hindu metaphysics—and all of Session 3.

～

The event is in the hand of God.

In 1787, just before the Constitutional Convention, George Washington met informally with delegates from several states. At this point, any future was still possible, from monarchy (with Washington himself as King George I) to an every-state-for-itself anarchy. These were the classic centripetal and centrifugal tendencies whose agon would go on to underlie American democracy. Washington heard the delegates chewing over all sorts of compromises, half-measures, and betrayals of the ideal that motivated the successful war against Britain. According to Gouverneur Morris, Washington spoke of striving for a Constitution, and a country, that would have all the radical nobility of that ideal.

> It is too probable that no plan we propose will be adopted. Perhaps another dreadful conflict is to be sustained. If, to please the people, we offer what we ourselves disapprove, how can we afterwards defend our work? Let us raise a standard to which the wise and honest can repair. The event is in the hand of God.

Here, independently of the Gita, we find another uncommonly wise soldier-statesman living the same attitude toward action. Washington, too, sought to "hold people together"—what the Gita calls *lokasamgraha*. Washington wanted the Convention of 1787 to focus on the ideal action itself, a dharmic action that would sustain the society. And he, too, exhorted Morris and the other delegates not to focus on the outcome. The outcome—the "event"—was not in their hands. Only the raising of the standard.

Like Krishna's, Washington's ethics concerned not just what to do or what not to do. He cared equally *how* the work was done. In the run-up to the momentous work—in Philadelphia as on Kurukshetra—both Washington and Krishna identified the root problem: Focusing too hard on the end result was stifling the necessary action. Their exhortations, though phrased in the languages of two different religious traditions, are identical.

Krishna recounts an impossible guru-student lineage: He places himself before the Sun God, Vivasvat, in time. At this still early point in the Gita, Arjuna thinks of Krishna as a friend but knows he is much more (though the great revelation of his friend's true nature is still several sessions away).

When Arjuna, perplexed by this lineage, asks Krishna what he means by this assertion of precedence, he does so respectfully—using the formal "you," the equivalent of *vous* in French. (Contemporary English, secularized and democratized, has forsaken the word for *Thou.*) Krishna explains that he and Arjuna have a history. Krishna remembers his past lives, which include all the avatars of Vishnu, most recently, Rama. Arjuna, like the rest of us, lives his life with no memory of his long biography. If he did, he would see how his own past works, good or ill, justify every new occurrence in his life—much like the "work" or steps preceding a mathematical solution. In Hinduism, what looks like chance is really causality, too complex to process for any mind but a God's.

This underlies the question the fourth session sets out to answer. As Krishna himself phrases it—*what is action?*

꙰

"Even poets," he notes, are confused about this. (Poets, let us not forget, were the original theologians.) The metaphor by which the Gita explains action is sacrifice.

The word *sacrifice,* or *yagna,* is meant to conjure a very specific image. The main Vedic religious ritual, which most modern-day Hindus experience most intimately during their weddings, has a fire at the center of it. The Brahmin chants and pours the offering into the fire. The fire is thought of as the "mouth" of the God or Gods, and the Gods "eat" the sacrifice. You are supposed to set aside a portion of everything you eat (and, metaphorically, do) for the Gods. There is a verse in Session 3 that talks about this: You do this to feed them and *to keep them alive.* Our Gods depend, for their existence, on our refusal to let them starve away.

‌

Acting in the world gets your hands dirty: in Arjuna's case, with the blood of his relatives. Metaphorically, that blood is sinful—the bad karma that will keep Arjuna from advancing toward Brahman.

How can Krishna reconcile the two ideals—worldly action, and otherworldly transcendence? Civil war, and inner peace?

There has to be some way to continue performing action while not accumulating karma. To become like the Gods themselves, who are not "smeared" with karma. The actions this war demands of Arjuna will be horrific. Krishna explains how to ground their karmic charge in Brahman: or better yet, how to burn away the actions, and their associated karma, entirely.

The trick is to make every action a *yagna,* a sacrifice. Spiritual knowledge makes every action a sacrifice, a series of ritual actions. The "fire of knowledge," at the center of the metaphorical mandala, reduces those actions to ashes. No actions, no karma.

As Krishna explains, every part of the sacrifice—the priest, the offering, the fire—is Brahman. By this poetic logic, Arjuna spilling the blood of his enemies is no different than a priest pouring ghee into the sacrificial fire.

The Gita consistently uses epithets for Fire, whether

pavaka, "purifier," or *vahnir,* "carrier" (implicitly carrying things *away*). These would have been awkward to jam into a translation, but their significance is clear: The mouth of Agni, God of Fire, will consume Arjuna's violent action, will purify it, will carry the bad karma away.

༄

I created four castes. . . .

I want to talk about the caste system. When a non-Hindu sees the word *Hinduism,* I suspect caste is one of the first things he or she thinks of. So let me first assert that it's possible to be a Hindu and repudiate India's caste system. I, and hundreds of thousands of Hindu Americans (and Hindu Indians) like me, are living examples of that. But I believe it's still important for me to think and write about this. After all, if the only part of the world where my coreligionists have been in the majority enshrined this system, and if it's mentioned pretty clearly in our scriptures, it strikes me as inappropriate to look away simply because it's not *essential* to living the religion.

I don't think it's enough, either, to point out that India's caste system was how a more or less universal human contradiction manifested itself. No one's history is a secret from anybody else. Our ideologies and religions conceive of equality, but our societies are always—and I mean *always* literally—unequal. European Christianity, both Catholicism and Protestantism, existed in conjunction with the Atlantic slave trade abroad and aristocracies at home. Orthodox Christianity, in Russia, had no problems with serfdom. Islam preached "brotherhood" and promptly established, in the original Caliphate, one of the largest slave-running operations of its day. Non-Muslims found themselves in a hierarchy, with "People of the Book" (Jews and Christians) above the infidel polytheists (like yours truly), but all subordinate to the rightly guided believers.

American democracy was built by slave labor; the Founding Fathers, for all those fine phrases at the beginning of the Declaration of Independence, created an oligarchy for landowning white males. *Liberté, égalité, fraternité* culminated in Napoleon grabbing his crown from the fingers of the Pope and setting it on his own head; the latest gospel of equality, Marxism, transferred power from a czar to a Stalin.

Is this all some primate reflex toward hierarchy, wired deep in us? We dream of equality, yet we organize ourselves into hierarchies. Or might this just be how large groups work?

The Gita explains both our differences and our sameness. It acknowledges the different classes of people and the different work they do in the world, but it asserts their underlying, metaphysical sameness. The Gita refuses to lump all of humankind into an in-group of believers and an out-group of infidels. While he makes no division into "believer" and "nonbeliever," Krishna proclaims our multiplicity in multiple ways, separating people according to the three gunas, or the four castes, or the two "inheritances."

Even as he describes this multiplicity of people, though, he describes their essential equality—in fact, their *unity*. It's not a contradiction for Krishna to say, in Session 4, "I created four castes" and then, in Session 5, to say, "Brahman is faultlessly egalitarian." The two assertions must not be considered separately. Separate them, and all manner of cruelty becomes possible. The differences among people—whether in their natures, or their "own work," *svakarma*—are divinely created. Because their true, spiritual identity is also divinely created, there are differences *but no inequalities*. In other words, Krishna introduced differences among people; human beings attached relative values to these differences, introducing inequality.

Several things start to make sense once we understand that these ideas are conjoined. First, the perfect willingness of Vishnu to dive into avatars other than the "high-est" Brahmin caste. Krishna is a *kshatriya,* or warrior, just like Rama. Before Krishna's avatar came a Fish, a Tortoise, a Boar: This most radically egalitarian perspective draws animals into its realm of identification. This is why Hindus have a sacred animal; "pagan" religions commonly regarded a given grove, tree, river, bird, or beast as sacred. From that perspective, a cow—or a golden sculpture of a calf—might well be considered worthy of reverence and celebration. Wise eyes could see the atman (which is to say, Brahman) even in a pig. Or, as the Gita puts it in Session 5:

> *A wise and cultured Brahmin,*
> *A cow, an elephant,*
> *A dog, a man who* cooks *dog:*
> *Scholars see them all the same.*

In that verse, Krishna is intentionally mentioning those that society considers subordinate or unclean. What's crucial is that he can find examples; society wasn't functioning correctly *then,* either. (If it were, the civil war wouldn't have been taking place.) He is speaking against that hierarchy. Differences are everywhere, but there's no reason to perceive those differences as unequal.

That is why only *tamas,* Darkness, gives gifts out of contempt (Session 17). Contempt arises when we internalize the hierarchy. It is an emotion we direct "down." People do different work because everybody has his or her own dharma (*svadharma*). One person translating this scripture and another person laying tile and a third person flying a plane aren't in a competition. There is no reason to rank us. Either we do right or do wrong or do not do. There is no work that is inherently better than any other. To understand Brahman is to understand the equality of all who constitute it.

Notice that even when the Gita lays out unflattering differences, like Darkness (*tamas*) or the demonic inheritance, the yogi is never enjoined to chastise, slaughter, enslave, or otherwise clobber people who possess these characteristics. This, the Gita is saying, is just how people are: various, but on a continuum, and striving to transcend it. Krishna never exhorts his human followers to punish. He appropriates to himself alone (see Session 16) the right to punish them, through rebirth.

Let me make something clear: None of this is an apologia for the historical cruelties of the caste system in India. I am not justifying Indian social practices. I am explaining the Gita—and how the Gita tried (and failed) to take the hierarchy out of multiplicity. It tried to do so by teaching the unity between the atman and Brahman. The most recent Hindu to learn this lesson fully, and live it fully, was Mahatma Gandhi. The rest of us are striving.

This is the first time Arjuna points out Krishna's tendency to praise two opposed or irreconcilable things. There may even be a note of frustration in that "definitely," *suniscitam,* with which he ends the opening question. Do I renounce all action, or do I pursue yogic action? Which is it? Session 5 consists of this one, four-line question followed by a long answer from Krishna.

Naturally, given the context, Krishna's preference is for the active yogi. He reconciles the seemingly irreconcilable through one of the Gita's central insights. Krishna explains how a yogi can act (and how, by extension, an archer can shoot) without letting the sin of the action "smear" him.

The key is to let go of the fruits, or results, of the action. You have to shift all the emphasis onto the action itself.

This is, almost incidentally, also a key to human happiness. (The Sanskrit word for happiness, *sukham,* occurs more than once in this session.) When you take your focus off the action at hand and put it on the results, you link your emotions to the future, which is out of your control.

The Gandiva bow and arrow are in Arjuna's hands—or *were,* before he threw them down in despair. Only the course of the arrow is in his control. The deaths of his Kaurava adversaries, as Krishna will explain later, are not. Arjuna's dharma is to make war on Kurukshetra. That is where he must focus: on the bird in hand, not on the weather next week.

Incidentally, that throwing down of bow and arrow in Session 1 has a connection to this session. *Samnyasa,* translated here as "renunciation" in keeping with most other translations of the Gita, has a closer etymological equivalent in *rejection. Rejection* has a Latin root that means "to throw," just as *samnyasa* has a sense of "to throw down" or "to cast aside." I opted against *rejection* because it doesn't quite fit; its connotations are off; and *renunciant,* while rare enough in English, is at least literary English, unlike *rejector. Samnyasa* is also the final stage of the idealized Hindu life—a final phase of old age when, children fathered and raised and the wealth passed on, a man casts away every last connection to his life. He leaves his worldly life behind him like a snakeskin. He is all lived out. This Sanskritic image has a clear connection to the Western idea of "renouncing" the world. So the common choice—even though it comes from the Latin *nuntiare,* "to report, to announce, to deliver a message," a *nuncio* being a papal ambassador—strikes me, alas, as the best one.

Of course, you can't be *completely* unaware of the results of your actions. That kind of willed ignorance is not advisable or even possible. Imagine an Arjuna who shoots his arrows without checking his target. You can keep the results clearly in mind; the point is to redirect your focus and your hope. You should hope to do the work well. You should not hitch your hope to the rewards that the work, if done well, will bring you.

Consider this translation. If I kept myself totally unaware of the existence of readers, I wouldn't write anything in the first place. But I must admit, even as I translated Session 5, even as I write this guide to it, that I do desire people to read what I am typing. I would love for the tapping action of my fingers to bear that "fruit." Yet my focus, dear reader, is not on you. If it were, I might massage the translation to make it more "accessible," or soft-pedal the metaphysics and present the Gita as a self-help book (it's only a matter of time before someone does that successfully). Instead, I keep my focus on the work itself as I do this, and it takes its own shape, line by line. What a literary critic or Sanskritist says, or how many stars an on-line reviewer gives it, is none of my concern. That is what makes the work possible in this form. That is what will keep it, no matter what evil is said or thought about it, "unsmeared."

This session presents the classic image of the yogi, serenely sitting in lotus position with hooded eyes crossed, the spine perfectly upright, at once balletic and still. The description even details how he prepares his seat. This idealized yogi is one of the earliest Indian images of religious enlightenment, dating back to the Upani-shads and before. It has become familiar to many in the West—either from yoga class or from images of the seated Buddha.

That ideal was originally Hindu, and it didn't have that much to do with various yoga-studio asanas from Down-ward Dog on down. That form of yoga, "Hatha-yoga," developed later. Krishna makes no mention of it. For him, yoga is ethical and spiritual. I imagine that the more physi-cal Hatha-yoga might have developed as a response to this seated pose—for the same reason today's sedentary office workers jump on the treadmill (or go to yoga class) after work.

❧

In two successive verses, Krishna proliferates a word. He has done this before. Last time, it was *Brahman,* and this time, *self.* So many *self*s bewilder us at first, just as so many *Brahman*s did then, and it can seem like a tongue-twisting tautology at first glance.

The image makes sense when you think of the essential unity of self and Brahman—and of Arjuna gazing out at the two armies. A yogi confronting the "self" resembles a soldier facing an enemy in battle: hostility on both sides, until the surrender . . . but after that, clemency on one side, cooperation on the other. Once you defeat your own selfishness, you are no longer self-serving. You are your own master, and the self is your helpmate.

While Krishna conjures this exalted ideal of the yogi, always emphasizing self-control and self-restraint, Arjuna feels less and less worthy of fancying his own face on that idealized, seated yogi.

Why would he? Consider the memories in Arjuna's mind. See him taking part in an archery competition as a boy, showing up his Kaurava cousins. See him setting a fire in the Khandava Forest, and the wild twisting death throes of the serpents and demons that burned to death in it. See him and his four brothers sitting, passive and shocked, around a game board, that fateful Game of Dice in which the Pandavas gambled and lost their kingdom to Prince Duryodhan. . . . Arjuna has acted and refrained from action in his life, but he has been far from a yogi.

This realization prompts his question. With meditative yoga being so difficult, what happens to someone who fails at it? A yogi dismisses worldly ambitions in favor of this higher one, but success isn't a given. In fact, it's a lot easier to get fame or money or glory than it is to unite with Brahman. You put all your metaphorical eggs in this one metaphysical basket: Now what?

Krishna assures Arjuna that no effort is lost. The system of rebirth ensures that he will take birth again and pick up where he left off. Krishna says this rebirth takes place after a temporary sojourn in heaven. This conception of the afterlife is yet another instance of the pluralistic Gita having it both ways at once. The belief in reincarnation is coupled with a belief in heaven and hell. It's just that, in the Gita, neither heaven nor hell is eternal. That certainly seems fairer than judging someone on a few years of life, then packing him or her off to one place or the other *forever*.

It isn't just mercy, though. Using time to limit death is how the frame story can continue. That frame story is the same for every living being: the atman's progress toward, *into,* Brahman. According to the Gita, people get the re-births they have earned; after death, they get the heaven or hell they deserve, for the length of time they deserve to get it; but every inch of progress toward Brahman carries over from rebirth to rebirth. The births and afterlives are episodes. The yogi's progress is the frame story. Those epi-sodes have the same theme as the frame story: justice.

More than once, over the course of Session 7, Krishna refers to knowing things whole, in their entirety, without remainder, without exception. There is a pun here, repeated elsewhere, on his own name. The term *kṛtsna* sounds almost exactly like his own name, and it means *entire*. The pun is meaningful. Whole knowledge is to know the entirety, and the entirety is synonymous—and nearly homophonous—with Krishna.

Krishna is all. This entirety allows for a generosity rarely seen in other scriptures: the broad-minded assurance that the worship of this or that *other* God is perfectly valid. This applies to the Vedic or Hindu pantheon, which was the only one known on the subcontinent at the time. In the modern day, however, the wisdom could apply to other traditions, too. Krishna explains that whatever good things come of their worship actually come from himself. This is not the attitude of a threatened or insecure deity. In the immense body of Krishna stories, from his childhood to his death, he experiences the gamut of human emotions, but he is never wrathful or irritable.

❧

Notice how little emphasis the vast Hindu myth-hoard places on Krishna's death. Different religions place varying degrees of emphasis on the deaths of their central figures. Christianity makes the death of Christ the hinge of history; to find the marvels and miracles of his childhood, we have to seek out the purged, apocryphal gospels. While the Prophet Mohammed's death, of fever, bears little emphasis, Shia Islam does glorify the far more spectacular death of

Ali. These fixations on death translate readily into the cult of the martyr, the glorification of the *shaheed*.

In Hinduism, the deaths of Rama and Krishna are almost afterthoughts. The childhoods of both figures burgeon with tales. So do their youths and adulthoods, which are literally epic tales of love and war. But the Hindu imagination took no interest in their deaths. In both cases, the death scenes are quite anticlimactic. Rama wades into a river—about as symbolic a gesture as you are likely to come up with. Krishna gets shot in the heel by a hunter. (A skeptical mind might sense a failure of invention here; this story bears a suspicious resemblance to Achilles getting shot in the heel by Paris.) Most tellings of the story rush to point out Krishna died by his own wish. He used the wound as an excuse to decamp.

Clearly the ancient Indians genuinely believed in the atman's immortality and in Vishnu's certain return. A sense of continuity across lives kept Hinduism away from any glorification of death, either of an avatar or of an individual. Even the Goddess Kali, with her necklace of skulls, is a lively dancer.

*

Krishna ends this session with a series of jargon words. They may look and sound strange to you—as they should, because they also seem strange to Arjuna. In fact, the very next session is going to open with his questions about them.

The first task of translation is finding a way to sound as little like a translation as possible while still maintaining accuracy. The terms that Arjuna asks about gave me great trouble. They consisted of familiar terms—self, God, being, sacrifice—but linked to a prefix that made them specific theological terms which have no English equivalent. The solutions of other translators, from direct transliteration of each term into Roman script (Sargeant) to "material manifestation" (Prabhupada) to "elemental-basis" (Feuerstein), were not for me. I decided I would carry out a process in English identical to the one carried out in the ancient Sanskrit. After all, these were not terms used in the everyday parlance or poetry of ancient India. They were theological terms, unusual enough that Arjuna asks Krishna to define them. So I hooked the familiar word to the equivalent English prefix. *Adhi* and *meta* are similar, and both have theological connotations. So if *metaself, metagod, metabeing,* and *metasacrifice* seem neither spoken nor poetic English but more like theological jargon, that is because I'm staying faithful to the original Gita.

～

Sanskrit is notorious for the way a given word has many meanings. In a particularly decadent, "late" period of its poetry, entire poems were written as elaborate double entendres—that is, two different poems made of the exact same words.

One such word has led my translation to deviate a bit from others. This word is *purusha*. Over time, this word has accrued several meanings. It can mean "sentience," or human consciousness, or any number of similar-sounding concepts. In some places in the Gita, Krishna uses this word to mean the highest goal to be attained. In the line *param purusha divyam,* the word *param* means "highest" and *divyam* means "divine." Yet in contemporary Gujarati, *purusha* can be used, simply, to mean "man."

Purusha's simultaneity—the way it can mean something essentially human or essentially divine—is the reason I made a point to juxtapose, where I could, its human and divine aspects. After all, the Gita's ideal future for the individual human atman projects it rejoining, or becoming, Brahman.

Hence "human godhood." The inherently divine nature of the atman is coded into this Sanskrit word, and its translation ought to span the extremes, too. The word means both things the same way the atman itself is both things: human and divine.

Purusha is by no means the only word that presents this issue. *Bhuta,* for example, can mean "being," "spirit," "creature," "species," "ghost." . . . Is it any surprise that Sanskrit, the language of polytheism, is polysemic?

❧

This session concludes with some lines about the time of death. It's important to keep two things in mind about Krishna's assertions here. Whether you or I will be reborn or not does not depend on the time of year we die, the first six months or the second six months. What Krishna says applies only to yogis, who are said to have control over their own deaths. They are capable of *svicchamrityu,* "self-willed-death." Just as bodhisattvas in Buddhism are enlightened souls who stay behind by choice, the yogi can come back for another birth by choosing his time of death in the latter half of the year. Krishna associates that death with the moon—the moon that wanes and disappears, but then waxes again; the moon in whose blotches ancient Hindus saw a rabbit, symbol there, too, of fertility.

The yogi who does not want to get reborn decides to die under the sign of the sun and, most tellingly, of fire. Fire, at the center of the sacrificial mandala, is the mouth of the God. The yogi, in a sense, is "consumed" by that fire. Once eaten, he is digested. Food, digested, becomes part of its eater. In the same way, a yogi—consumed, assimilated, consummated—ends up as a permanent part of the Permanent.

This session makes a point of describing the wisdom and the secret as *royal*. Toward the end as well, Krishna mentions kings who reach a level of sainthood. An Indian example is the father of Princess Sita from the *Ramayana:* King Janaka was Krishna's own father-in-law from a prior incarnation. The European Christian equivalent would be France's Louis IX or Hungary's Stephen I, both canonized; India's King Asoka is considered an enlightened ruler in the Buddhist tradition. The mention of royalty brackets Session 9, hinting at Krishna's highest dream for Arjuna—that Arjuna might go on to become not just a victor on Kurukshetra but a *rajarishi* or "king-seer" himself.

The session begins and ends on telling personal notes. Krishna confides the "royal secret" because his friend will not scoff or sneer. The Godsong is delicate; the listener must be open to it. It isn't just the God who must be willing to connect. The session ends with an exhortation to devotion and an assurance that it will not be in vain. That final assurance contrasts with the vain hopes, works, and knowledge of those who put "no faith in dharma."

Between these personal notes, though, Krishna waxes expansive. He speaks of producing and rendering extinct, cyclically, the whole plethora of living species; he identifies himself, systematically, as every part of the traditional fire sacrifice, and the three major Vedic scriptures. (You will notice he does not mention the fourth Veda, the Atharva, which joined the Vedic corpus in the second half of the first millennium B.C.)

In this expansive mood, Krishna also proclaims his agency in the weather, and asserts himself as the cause of being, and declares himself the ultimate recipient of the worship of *other* Gods, too. That may sound like insufferable presumption to the jealous or infidel-hating God of many another scripture, but the Gita insists, never more clearly than this, on the trivial distinction between polytheism and monotheism from the perspective of Brahman.

It's that perspective, incidentally, that explains this expansiveness. Krishna is speaking, more frankly than ever, in the voice of his simultaneous, divine nature. The mask of the human slips; the God is showing. He is about to show this even more unabashedly. The escalating assertions of Session 9 are a preview of the poetic and, finally, literal dilations of Sessions 10 and 11.

Arjuna's questions, until now, have been a student's. His curiosity has been ethical, philosophical, metaphysical. Now, for the first time, his curiosity is personal. He inquires after the stranger inside his friend. Krishna has made it impossible not to wonder.

Addressing Krishna, Arjuna, in the first line he speaks in Session 10, twice uses the word *param,* "highest" or "supreme." This idea of supremacy informs Krishna's answer. His answer takes the familiar form of a catalogue, another feature of the heroic epic that finds its way, transfigured, into the Gita. Homer catalogues ships; the poet of the Gita catalogues the splendors of the universe. Walt Whitman would use this poetic technique centuries later in *Leaves of Grass* to express grandeur in all its details, the one self in all its multiplicity. Session 10 is the pre-echo of "Song of Myself."

Krishna's first-person singular voice diffracts, polytheistically, into other deities: He locates himself in the Gods of money and desire, for example. He even names two prior avatars of Vishnu. Abstractions, like Time and Death, crowd into the list. Still, the dominant mode is pantheistic, naming individual people, mountains, seasons, trees, and animals, both mythical and real.

Metaphysically, of course, divinity dwells in every creature, of every species. The splendor specific to each, the "highest" of each kind, is Krishna. His height is the limit to which each kind aspires. This holds true of people as well: Arjuna implies as much, calling Krishna *purusottam,* "Highest Man."

As for the people Krishna mentions, many of the names are historical, like Kapila, the philosopher who founded Samkhya. Some are so far in the past as to be almost legendary, like the ancient priest Brihaspati, after whom Indian astronomers later named a planet. Still other names are ones that Arjuna has heard only in stories about the Gods, like Skanda, the son of Shiva and Parvati. (It is no small reassurance that, by Krishna's poetic logic, Arjuna's charioteer is none other than the War God himself.)

Krishna names all three kinds of names with perfect familiarity. It's as if an ancient Greek were to speak of being the historic philosopher Plato, the distant figure of Orpheus, and the war god Ares; or, in the Biblical tradition, of being Aquinas, Aaron, and the archangel Michael. Arjuna realizes with a thrill that his friend has been and will be present everywhere, from myth to prehistory to history to now to eternity.

Eventually Krishna tires of his catalogue. He knows it could go on forever, and now that he has begun to reveal himself, he gets impatient with words. This is an idea unique, as far as I know, to the Gita: Here, and only here, the mystery is *eager* to be understood. To tell is to proliferate verses. It would be much more effective to *show*.

Which brings us to Session 11.

Arjuna asks to see what he has heard about. What follows is one of the climactic sequences in the Gita, the Vision of the Universal Form.

Once asked, Krishna reveals himself in his entirety—but in the poem, it's implied that Arjuna reacts with a dumbfounded stare into space. That is why Krishna realizes that his friend cannot see the Vision with regular, human eyes. "I'll give you a *divine* eye." It's a very human false start of this friend overeager to let his friend in on a Secret.

Dante, in the final canto of the *Paradiso,* speaks of *la forma universal,* the exact Italian equivalent of the Sanskrit *vishwa-rupa.* The *Commedia*'s Vision reconciled an abstract Trinity with the divine-human body of Jesus. So in Canto 33, Dante sees, initially, a radiance, just as Arjuna does. Then Dante sees a circle that has three colors; after that, in some way he says he cannot fully describe, he sees our human likeness, *la nostra effige,* radiating out of that circle, or around it.

Dante presents a geometrical Vision. Its human aspect is only vaguely adumbrated. The *Commedia* ends with Dante trying and failing to puzzle out how the human "effigy" emerges from that radiant, tricolored circle. Other monotheistic Visions, before Dante's, refrained from mixing human imagery and the divine. Moses sees and hears a burning bush; the Book of Job presents a meteorological Vision, with its voice inside a whirlwind; the Prophet Mohammed sees the archangel Gabriel, but his direct experience of the divine is purely auditory, devoid of imagery. In all three cases, the human element is limited to language.

The Gita's Vision, in love with multiplicity, explodes with language, light, and human bodies. This Vision is the most vibrantly polytheistic part of the Gita. More is more.

Everything crowds into this expanded Form at once, the whole universe "standing here as one." Krishna's human body diffracts, prismatically, into an infinite number of body parts. Arjuna sees not just dazzling light but arms, bellies, mouths, eyes. The Gita's image reconciles abstract, philosophical Hinduism (the radiance) with the Hinduism of the pantheon (the human bodies). It reconciles the sublime formulas of the Upanishads and the anthropomorphic deities of mythology and popular worship. The Gita even manages to reconcile polytheism and monotheism: The divine form and the human form are the same thing because the divine Brahman and the human atman are one. It's just that the oneness takes the form of multiplicity.

This unabashedly polytheistic Vision codes itself into the very structure of the verse. The first words of six lines early on in the description are *aneka, aneka, aneka, divyam, divyam, divyam*. Many, many, many, divine, divine, divine. I made a point to preserve this exactly. This word *many,* in Sanskrit, is, technically, "not-one." It is a preemptive rebuke to the monotheistic credo, though understandable as such only in retrospect. Krishna and the Gita-poet both were blissfully unaware of the Bible's contempt for polytheism, blissfully prior to the Qur'an's hatred of polytheists. Singling out a way of worship, or a way of conceiving the divine, as evil and deserving of aggression—this is one of the few things not to be found in the Gita's everything-at-onceness.

‿

Arjuna's stunned awe gives way to terror. This universe, though full of recognizably human forms, does not itself recognize human "good" and human "evil." After marveling awhile, Arjuna sees horrific images of death, the warriors around him vacuumed into all these mouths, their heads stuck between chomping teeth. Time means nothing from the perspective of the universe. Krishna says he has already killed the people Arjuna is going to kill. What Arjuna thinks he should not do has already happened. The arrows will glide through preexisting tunnels in the air.

This grotesque cruelty is an aspect of the Universal Form, too. The eyes above those faces do not see such mass death as grotesque or cruel. They are indifferent. That is why Arjuna begs Krishna to make it stop, to resume a human form. Arjuna, who at the beginning of this session asked to see, at the end of it asks *not* to see. He asks Krishna to cover up the glowing/glowering multiplicity of the Universal Form with the mask of a single familiar face. And Krishna complies.

This is the shortest chapter in the Gita. Krishna's body is the same as before, only utterly estranged. Krishna has fanned and shivered the universe like a peacock. From now on, he will always hide this possibility.

The new estrangement does not silence, rather it fosters Arjuna's questioning. The first question that occurs to him concerns how best to meet again that Stranger he glimpsed in his friend. He has heard about a multiplicity of ways to get to the same place.

Krishna's answer epitomizes the multiplicities of the Gita. He understands that different people have different temperaments; some like singing together in a crowd, others like ladling out soup for the homeless, while still others like reading (and translating) ancient scriptures. Still others like a combination of these. Krishna offers method after possible method.

Just as he acknowledges different temperaments and tendencies, he acknowledges different capabilities. His priority is reunion with whoever loves him. So he goes down a list from most difficult (the contemplation of a divine abstraction) to the very easiest (total surrender, coupled with self-restraint).

He finishes out with another portrait of the ideal devotee. This is a common theme of the Gita: Unlike many other scriptures that spend their time praising the divine, the Gita spends a lot of time, in session after session, praising the ideal devotee. This may be because the individual atman, as it approaches through yoga the asymptote of its being, *becomes* Brahman. *Tat tvam asi:* I imagine a sage in saffron pointing at the heavens with one hand and at me with the other, shouting, "That's *you!*"

To praise one is to praise the other.

﹏

A personal note, if I may, about devotion.

I had my first sense of a "false god" at a concert once, surrounded by what felt like a thousand lifted cigarette lighters. I thought of the candles set before an altar I had seen some years before, in a church in France. This, I thought, is what those scriptures were talking about: frenzy, reverence, devotion, directed—*mis*directed—toward a mere singer of songs. These responses, at this intensity, were the rightful due of the divine. Only a God deserved this frenzy, this reverence, this devotion, because a God did more than entertain you. A God elevated your conduct and your thinking.

The polytheist in me interpreted the monotheistic scriptures in this way for some time. I took "Thou shalt have no other Gods before me" to mean "Don't worship celebrities." Dancing around the golden calf meant, to me, working for the sake of wealth and fame. I took "infidels" to mean the people, seemingly in the millions, who had no particular religion and burned with devotion for sports figures or actors or musicians (or, among "highbrows," for poets and artists).

My thinking changed with time and study. What were these celebrity-worshipping "infidels" responding to? The beauty of a body's movement or the power of a mind's. *Yoga is finesse in action.* The smiling power forward spinning the ball on his finger might mirror, *iha loke,* here in the world, a God supporting the spinning earth. Music *was* a Mystery, wasn't it? It communicated independently of its placeholder lyrics. As I knew from experience, the sung text didn't have to be a prayer or a sermon for the musically mediated, inward transfiguration to take place. Why not revere the human being who communicated it to you? Artists of any kind are apertures. Through them, we glimpse "expansive glories." If Brahman is atman, the divine is human, and the human, too, is divine—if only in snatches on the court or stage, or holding a guitar, or at a laptop assembling lines of poetry.

But that explained only the *reason* for the devotion. Was devotion to a God, or to yoga, better? And if yes, why?

I believe that the highest devotion is the one that makes demands on us. It says: *Do this,* or *Do this differently.* It also says: *Don't do that,* or, in a more familiar form, *Thou shalt not.* But most consistently, it whispers that line of Rilke's that became one of my mantras: *Du musst dein Leben andern.* You must change your life.

The right human apertures on the divine, I thought, might change my life. I would devote myself only to people who would make demands on me, goad me to discipline myself, behave selflessly, become better. I went on to gain four such divinely human objects of devotion: my wife, my twin sons, and my daughter.

Fostering each other,
You will attain the highest good.

This session begins with a request from Arjuna that seems to hint at private study, incomplete and unsatisfying. Warriors in that era had Brahmins as preceptors, and their training, especially in the case of the Pandavas, was theological as well as martial. They were not quite the equivalent of Loyola's Jesuits, but they were not Homeric brutes, either. Among the best of the *Mahabharata* warriors, martial spirit and spiritual martiality blended, as they did among the ancient samurai. This is why Arjuna can ask a question that begins with very technical terms—*prakriti* and *purusha*—and connect them to a metaphorical "Field" and "Knower of the Field."

I have translated *purusha* elsewhere differently; here, the context of the Field and the Knower of the Field demands a different English word. Session 13 pairs *Purusha* with *Prakriti* throughout. *Prakriti* is mere materiality, and *Purusha* what experiences and navigates it. Notice, however, the alliteration between these two words in the original Sanskrit. They are distinct but entangled, and that entanglement is reflected at the level of consonant sounds. Hence my choice, for *Purusha* and *Prakriti,* of *Sentience* and *Substance.*

As in other sessions, Krishna recounts the qualities of an ideal human being. In this session, one of his longest lists defines the knowledge that makes for a "Knower of the Field."

∾

In one *sloka* (17), a little prestidigitation was necessary on my part. I feel compelled to "show my work" on this one, if only to point out how ingenious the Sanskrit can get.

The Vishnu who nourishes species,
Known as their devourer and evolution

The original *sloka* hides a piece of complex verbal signaling. Basically, Krishna is saying that the force that nourishes species—Krishna-as-Vishnu, the Sustainer God—is simultaneously their Creator and Destroyer. This is signaled, in the Sanskrit, by a deliberate rhyme:

grasishnu prabhavishnu ca

Those are two words, occurring here and nowhere else, for Destroyer and Creator—literally, and alliteratively, "devourer" and "developer." As you can see for yourself, the second word, *prabhavishnu,* actually contains the name of Vishnu inside it. In one creation myth, Brahma emerges from the navel of Vishnu. The Sanskrit encodes the three-fold identity through the repetition of the *ishnu* sound for Creator and Destroyer, and by collapsing the name of the Sustainer into the name of the Creator. A pretty slick line—and definitely not an accident. I had to do something here.

First, I called the Sustainer God by the name that's "buried" in the original. I could have replicated the Gita's replication of the *ish* sound by "As their demolisher and establisher." (No words in English with the full *-ishnu* ending, alas.) While it's true we generally don't use the word *establisher* in English, the whole point would be to use a word for each of them that's not used anywhere else. I ended up doing this anyway, but not with those ungainly *ish* words.

What would be lost is the image of "devouring" that is present in *grasishnu.* That dovetails with the idea of the sacrificial fire devouring the offering, and the devouring mouths of Session 11. It's a major theme. After consideration, I gave more weight to that image than to the repeated *ish* sound. Instead of introducing a construction-destruction metaphor, which isn't present in the Gita, I carried over the eating metaphor intact. Simultaneously, I unpacked and emphasized the *Vishnu,* and I echoed the phonetic interconnectedness of the Sanskrit words by alliterating on *v* instead of *sh* for all three.

~

This session's "Field," the *kshetra,* dovetails with the very first line of the Gita, which repeats the word twice: *Dharmakshetre Kurukshetre.*

For Arjuna, becoming a "Knower of the Field"—the Field in any sense, physical or ethical—means becoming a better warrior and better man. What Krishna teaches is theological knowledge of the Field—and, metaphorically, martial mastery of the *battle*field.

Anyone who listens to the Gita can't help but notice how much time is spent on human beings. The Song is sung by a God about people and what they can become. What they can become is divine.

The Gita was written long before psychology became its own field. So the study of human motivation and personality—and their pathologies—was just one more branch of religious thought. (*Psyche* is a Greek word for "soul.") Krishna's Purity, Power, and Darkness don't exactly correspond to Freud's superego, ego, and id, but there are some uncanny resemblances in the two models. The human psyche exists as a combination of all three; one of the three can dominate the others, and a person's behavior will show it.

One of the first things to go in a psychiatric disorder is insight. This session of the Gita describes each guna and what it looks like when one or another predominates. This three-part way of dividing everything human will recur in subsequent sessions, especially the last one, as Krishna imposes a conceptual order on the motley tendencies of the human race.

This session also makes explicit the end point of knowing all this about the gunas: transcending them. Krishna tells Arjuna about the gunas to give Arjuna insight and help him overcome the bondage of being human.

Because all three of the gunas—even *sattva,* here translated as "Purity"—work against the ultimate goal of being human, which is becoming divine. Purity, for example, binds you to knowledge, even if it's "good" knowledge, like knowledge of a scripture such as this.

The Gita, early on, spent whole sessions on the various kinds of yoga, or ways of uniting with Brahman. Perhaps not coincidentally, these, too, were three in number: knowledge, action, and devotion.

Now the Gita will spend whole sessions on the three gunas, but the purpose is the same: to unite with Brahman. The first set of three details what you need to do; the second set of three, what you need to transcend.

What you need to transcend is human nature itself. The point of understanding the gunas is to go beyond the gunas, just as the point of understanding the Gita is to go beyond the Gita.

Where is that beyond? The Singer might point at his own heart, or at the heart of the friend to whom he sings. The point of discovering the ultimate Elsewhere is to discover it is Here.

This session opens with the Gita's longest extended metaphor—a surreal, upside-down tree, suspended in the sky. Unlike Dadaism, the Gita conjures this striking image programmatically, with every detail of the picture possessing a meaning. To understand Krishna's tree metaphor is to understand much of the Gita's conception of human life and its purpose.

After the tree, the session is straightforward and sublime: Krishna segues naturally from the tree to his role sustaining plant life and human life; the fire, or *agni,* is literally central to the Brahmin sacrifice, and the chemical fire of gastric acid ("metabolic fire") is central to the human body. The two sustaining roles are connected, too. The word for *herb* is *aushadi,* a word that implies a medicinal value and lives on in spoken Hindi and Gujarati to this day.

But about that tree.

Elements of the metaphor have puzzled translators and interpreters for centuries. At one point the roots are above, but some lines later, the roots are clearly stated as being below. The best explanations have come from those who have looked at an asvattha tree. Frequently the roots are highly individuated around the base and course visibly up the trunk, directly into the branches. They look thick and corded, like so many enormous Achilles tendons. That may be one explanation.

Another explanation requires us to visualize the tree's entire root system, without the obscuring earth. Imagine a tree completely uprooted and flipped. It flares into branches at both ends, top and bottom; only in one case, the branches are the roots. The reference may be figurative in the second instance—that is, the branches occupy the expected (lower) place of roots. A metaphor within the metaphor, as it were. Let's allow Krishna some poetic license and move on.

The asvattha tree is a conduit between the otherworldly and the worldly. It has its roots, or origin, in the heavens. Its leaves are Vedic hymns; to chant or read those Vedic hymns is to nourish the tree. We give those leaves the breeze of our breath, the sunlight of our gaze. The tree itself is "nourished by gunas," that is, by the fertile soil of human tendencies and desires. (Literature and art have no other soil.) The asvattha tree is a fig tree, and these sprouted fruits—always a loaded word in the Gita—are sweet things of the senses. Actions, too, here "below" on earth, get entangled in the wide sweep of the inverted tree, which brushes the ground of Kurukshetra.

Much is included in this metaphorical tree. The atman is meant to climb up this inverted tree, toward the heavens, then cut the tree down with "detachment's hard weapon." *Weapon* is the word that Krishna uses, not *axe;* Arjuna is not a lumberjack but a warrior. To fell that tree is to see it drop away, sweet sensory figs and green Vedic leaves and all.

From there, as Krishna explains, Arjuna must go above the celestial network of asvattha roots. That is where Arjuna can find Krishna—sustaining not just the tree but all of life.

This may be why Krishna describes his "highest home" as devoid of light, solar or lunar. It is located somewhere more profound than any root. Its darkness is at once on high and deep, celestial and subterranean.

~

Ficus religiosa has other names. Another name for the asvattha tree is the Bo tree—the very tree under which the Buddha went on to have his enlightenment. The historical "Blessed Lord" antedates the historical "Awakened One," but if we consider the Gita as a poem composed and inserted into the *Mahabharata,* we can guess at its historical date based on some internal evidence.

From this perspective, the Gita was written *after* the Upanishads (the same "Vedanta" Krishna mentions having crafted) but *before* the Atharva Veda joined the original three Vedas (Krishna always refers to the Vedas as three, not four). Historians have vague ideas about when each of those scriptures coalesced into its respective form. To elide the controversies a bit, the Gita may have been composed around or a little after the Buddha's enlightenment. It may well have been an answer to the challenge of Buddhism in India.

In this light, there is a bit of wordplay in the penultimate line of this arboreal session.

etad buddhva buddhiman syat

Is this a double entendre, doubled for effect? I chose to retain the word *Awakening* in the translation to honor this implication. If the Gita were truly written after the dissemination of Buddha's teachings, the Gita-poet's gesture of generosity is ahead of its time.

It would take centuries for the rivalry between these two religions to end, well beyond even the latest estimates of the Gita's composition date. Indian Buddhism converted its Constantine-equivalent in Asoka (ruled 268–232 B.C.), and Buddhism became the official religion of empire. It never managed to root out the religion that gave rise to it, just as Christianity and Islam could not break Judaism. Buddhism's quietus on the subcontinent came a millennium and a half later, with the arrival of Islam. Islamic armies destroyed Nalanda and the other Buddhist centers of learning and monasteries; they could not eradicate the decentralized, multitudinous Hinduism of peasants and village Brahmins.

Why is the Gita's gesture, if such it is, ahead of its time? Hinduism has a well-known assimilative tendency, and metaphysically (after Buddhism was out of the subcontinent and no longer a threat, I suspect), the rivalry ended in a very Hindu way: Hindus today consider the Buddha the penultimate avatar of Vishnu. Rama is Vishnu's seventh avatar, Krishna his eighth, the Buddha his ninth.

The Gita-poet gives more than one nod to the avatar *preceding* Krishna, referring to Rama's father-in-law by name, and to the monkey (Hanuman) on the banner of Arjuna; Krishna declared himself Prince Rama in Session 10. The Bo tree and wordplay in this session may well be two nods to Krishna's successor.

Of course, for every one Hindu who thinks the Gita was a poem composed circa 500 B.C.E. by an anonymous Brahmin and inserted into the *Mahabharata,* there are about a hundred thousand who think it the painstaking transcription by Vyasa of a conversation that really occurred during the Heroic Age, in meter. For those readers, this business about the tree and the double entendre is best considered coincidental—but, I trust, uncannily so.

As for myself, I almost never think about the date of the Gita's composition. When I do think about its chronology, I enjoy watching it take on different meanings, depending on where I slide it along the time line. The Gita, like any scripture, is perpetually timely, composing itself afresh in the reader or listener, even after repeated readings and listenings. Historical quibbling isn't just irrelevant when it comes to scripture; it's a buzz kill. A scripture welcomes the imagination to place it in any context and see how the moment demanded this timelessness. So I prefer to let my Gita float free of history and geography. It travels great distances without being diminished. What if the Gita had been composed in India, about a hundred years after the Buddha? An interesting enough question, but there are others just as interesting, if not more interesting. What if the Gita had been composed in Europe, in 1939? Or here in America, in 2001? Or right now?

The key Sanskrit word in this session is *sampadam*. You will find this word rendered, depending on the translator, as "destiny," "endowment," "qualities," and "nature." There are shades of all of these in the Sanskrit word. The 1899 *Sanskrit-English Dictionary* of Sir Monier Monier-Williams points out how the word comes from *sam + panna,* or "furnished with." And there are also instances in which this word has been used as "wealth" or "opulence."

The full meaning lies in the summation of those past English equivalents. *Nature* and *destiny,* specifically: Session 16 gives the sense of nature *being* destiny. The Gita begins by listing qualities, and then, in each case, divine or demonic, it mentions that whoever has them is born with them.

The many-minded Gita, recall, includes ways of thinking that conceive of things in singular or dualistic terms as well. In this discussion of contrasts, the divine *sampadam* or demonic *sampadam,* each present at birth, leads to certain traits manifesting in the adult. The Gita is referring to what we, today, would call genetic inheritance, those traits and predispositions with which each human being is born. This notion of heredity—of an "endowment" you are born with, for good or ill—guides my choice of "inheritance" for *sampadam*. It is a word which has not, to my knowledge, been used before in any translation of the Gita. The way I arrived at it may be tinged with modern science, but the justification, as I hope you can see, lies in the ancient Sanskrit itself.

～

One of the few outlooks missing from the Gita is the Utopian ideal: this runaway fantasy (in Session 16, the metaphorical Sanskrit is "mind-chariot") that, one day, if the right set of ideas is put into practice, *all* people will end up happy and productive in some workers' paradise, or singing in a choir in the kingdom of heaven on earth, or bowing clockwork-pious in the same direction.

The Gita is just too pragmatic for that. It believes human diversity is intractable. Not just in *svabhava,* someone's "own nature," and *svadharma,* someone's "own dharma," and not just in the group identities of tribe or caste (or nationality, or sect, or party . . .). Humanity's stubborn diversity includes innate qualities, an individual's divine or demonic "inheritance."

The Gita, and Hinduism generally, does not daydream about the perfectibility of *mankind.* It believes only in the perfectibility of the individual. And that occurs through the atman's homecoming—over many births, along "the highest path"—to Brahman.

Three is the first polytheistic number. Once you move beyond the monomaniacal one and get through the two of dualism, the road is clear, all the way to infinity. The major monotheistic traditions either destroyed three, as early Islam did the three pre-Islamic goddesses of Arabia, Al-Lat, Al-Manat, and Al-Uzza, or forced three into one, as early Christianity did through the doctrine of the Trinity.

The Gita revels in threes. Three is the manageable multiplicity by which the Gita orders the infinite world. Session 17 uses the three gunas to classify faiths and diets. It goes on to classify, again according to the three gunas, the varieties of religious acts. Religious acts are themselves of (surprise!) three kinds: sacrifice, austerity, and charity. There are different sorts of austerities, by the way—austerities of body, speech, and mind.

The session finishes by expanding a verbal gloss on Brahman. I use the word *gloss* purposefully: The phrase is not a name or definition, and unlike *"Neti neti,"* it is not a formula, either. The Gita calls it a *nirdesa,* and diligent hunting has found this word showing up in several ancient Sanskrit grammatical treatises, sometimes in the title, usually with the meaning of "exposition." The gloss of something is its paraphrase and gist, and *Aum Tat Sat* glosses Brahman. In three syllables.

_ _

I have saved some room here, in the next to last of these guides, to talk about our subject itself. I want to point out how much of "theology," "metaphysics," and "religious thought" is really just storytelling.

In Asia, the most widely disseminated story, found

everywhere from Indian television serials to the Javanese puppet theater, is a religious one, the *Ramayana*. Not for nothing do the Christians call the Gospels "the greatest story ever told." These are the stories that take the form of stories, with heroes, struggles, and happy or tragic endings, or else an ending that combines the tragic and the happy. Rama rules his kingdom justly for a long time—but does so alone, having exiled to the forest the very woman he fought Ravana to retrieve. The Crucifixion, too, is a hybrid ending: Jesus suffers and loses his life, but humankind gains a Savior. Storytelling—parable, myth, or mythistory—forms the body of religion.

But even a religion's more abstract ideas are just another kind of story. The plot is more suspenseful than any airport paperback's, and the hero is more sympathetic. *Where did I come from? What will become of me?* You are the protagonist. This is your origin story. You read to find out what happens to you.

You may believe the story that you are born once and will die once. What you do in that interval will determine where you go. If you were virtuous, you go to heaven for eternity (unless you were born before God's son died, in which case you end up in Limbo). If you were a sinner, you go to hell.

Or you may believe the story in which your people made a special Covenant with God. Or you may believe the story in which an Arab merchant became the last and most authoritative in a long line of (Jewish) prophets. Or else you may believe the story about the angel Moroni telling Joseph Smith about golden plates covered in ancient Egyptian writing buried in Ontario County, New York. The one-birth plotline also appeals to people who think they decompose into nitrogen and sustain plant life after they die. Christian, Jew, Muslim, Mormon, scientific materialist: They are defined by which set of stories makes sense to them.

I am a Hindu because I believe the story Hinduism tells about me. I have read enough accounts of Hinduism by non-Hindus (from the age before political correctness) to know that its ideas seem absurd, grotesque, or silly to others. But the Gita has told me its story about myself, and nothing else sounds right anymore.

My atman is a salmon, thrashing upstream to my source. The river it strives against consists of waterfall after waterfall, each one steeper than the next, until the last one, the one beyond which is Brahman. That last one is a Niagara. The river is rage and lust and greed; it's sloth and slacking; it's a finicky purity and the puritan's contempt for human failings: in other words, the three gunas of our natures, all of which, even Purity, work to keep my atman from reaching the "highest goal," Brahman. Every leap against the waterfall is a birth; every splashdown is a death.

I have cleared waterfalls to reach this human form. If I relent, I will be swept downstream. So I read and I write and I translate and I think and I do right by my family and I practice radiology and I strive always to pluralize myself because every life I live from here on out must be a salmon jump upstream to my source, to Brahman. I want to return there for good. I feel it is close, just up Niagara Falls over there. I am singing God's song to get ready. When I jump I will jump for joy.

After all that he has taught and shown, Krishna the charioteer has not let go of the reins—as though the whole song were a mere pause in the work to be done. Maybe both Krishna and Arjuna sense that the time has come to stop speaking and get to the bitter work of war.

Arjuna's question concerns the final phase of the traditional Hindu life, a retreat from the world and final renunciation, or *sannyasa*. This word, *sannyasa,* comes from a word that means "throwing down"—everything you own and treasure, cast off like the sand sacks from a hot-air balloon. Arjuna's confusion is understandable: He wants to know how this throwing down of the world differs from letting the world go in a philosophical sense—the difference between rejecting it and relinquishing it.

Krishna's answer is one of his lengthiest. He is trying to order the universe for Arjuna before they finish their talk. A simple contrast between the two forms of renunciation gives way to a discussion of the three gunas. Krishna lays out the threefold natures of work, will, intellect, knowledge, resolve, and happiness.

Three factors give way to four as Krishna moves on to the four castes. In this section, we see the original ideal of castes—which was not hierarchical, not some justification for one group to behave snobbishly or cruelly toward another. In fact, as Krishna explains it, caste acknowledges all the different roles of people as natural and fitting, parts of a societal ecosystem. His conception has its real-world analog in the Pandava Army behind him. That army is more than just its massed soldiers. It's the coolies who make up the train of the army, carrying equipment and supplies on their backs; the merchants who supply the army, for a price, immense quantities of buckles and axles and harnesses and horses and swords and hilts; the priests cracking coconuts against the wheels of each chariot, murmuring mantras, legitimizing the Pandava cause. None of the classes of people involved in the war effort resent their roles, no more than a foot soldier resents Arjuna's chariot and Gandiva bow. This army, this contained society, does not fester with rage at hierarchy and group enmities. They all know that any healthy collective life consists of many differences of function, but a unity of purpose.

~

At one point, Krishna says, "Do what you want to do. . . ." He seems to have finished speaking; for a moment, he waits for his friend to respond. When Arjuna doesn't answer, words rush out of Krishna—"Hear me out again"—only this time, his words are not philosophical. His words focus instead on their relationship. Worried, maybe, that cosmic visions and detailed teachings have not been enough to persuade his friend, Krishna looks him in the eyes and makes one last, personal appeal. "The secret of all secrets," he explains, is, simply, "I love you."

~

I love you. Why is this the "secret of all secrets"? After all these complex metaphysical discussions, all this Sanskrit poetry—*sancta simplicitas,* sacred simplicity. Or is this secret all that simple? This is the same love that Dante wrote of, the love "that moves the sun and the other stars." It is the same love that Rumi and the other Sufis meant when they wrote their poems to the Beloved. *For God so loved the world . . .* Here, at the end of the Gita, we have been taught how to understand love. We can place this love of Krishna for Arjuna, friend for friend, in its metaphysical context—along with filial love, the love between siblings, parental love, romantic love.

If Brahman and atman are the same, so are atman and atman, yours and that of the one you love. Atman experiences union with another atman, the boundary between them gone. Love's bliss is practice bliss for the yogic union of atman and Brahman. Two bodies seem like two separate beings, but love dispels that delusion, as any lover or parent knows, until physiology itself reflects the new unity. We know of these things happening, but we do not read enough into them. How a mother sometimes wakes up moments before the sleeping infant registers hunger. How a reflex will hurl a parent in front of an oncoming car to snatch her child out of danger. That unity can expand the definition of *self,* of *atman,* to include the people of your country, your faith, your race. Act accordingly, and you work toward the state of a Gandhi or a Martin Luther King, Jr. Beyond this lies identification with all humankind, and to live this *agape* transfigures the self, more effectively than sacramental bread and wine, into Christ. Beyond this lies identification with all living things. "I bring it all to be, / And from me, all evolves." And beyond even that, identifying with all things living and nonliving, the self unites, at last, with all of Being. With Brahman. This is the state the Godsong sings, and is, and sings us toward.

So when Krishna says he "loves" Arjuna, he means that between his "self" and Arjuna's "self" there is no barrier but delusion. Love can dissolve that barrier by reminding Arjuna of his origin, when he was at One, when he was still a song the Singer had not sung. When Arjuna answers,

nashto moha smritir labdha,

he is saying that he has lost his delusion and has gained—*re*gained—his memory. Love has taught him to remember who he always was.

ّ

I find it sweet that the God is unsure of himself at the end. His last lines to Arjuna in the poem are questions, desperately asking if all these verses are enough to dispel his doubts.

They are. Arjuna realizes the white horses are yoked to the chariot. The chariot is yoked to the will of the Charioteer. He realizes he must yoke himself to the Charioteer and go where he is driven, releasing arrow after arrow in the coming battle. All this talk of "yoking" and "release" has come down to these white horses yoked to this chariot, and the arrows on the ground that he alone must string and release.

"I will do what you command." At that, Krishna turns to the horses, and without so much as a shake of the reins, the chariot begins to move across the plain of Kurukshetra, back to the Pandava Army. The dust behind the chariot rises in a dense cloud, and this fills the sky.

ّ

When this cloud clears, we are at the court of King Dhritarashtra. Sanjaya is at his side as before.

We are back at the opening scene—but everything has changed. "My delusion has perished. My memory gains." Plato once wrote that what we call "learning" is really a way of reminding the soul of what it once knew. That is what the Gita has done for Arjuna; it has reminded him who he is. For centuries, the Gita has been reminding Hindus around the world who they are. This expansion of memory is an expansion of being, on the same scale as Krishna's in Session 11.

No wonder Sanjaya finishes out the Gita by telling the blind King that, having heard this Godsong, he remembers and remembers it—and that the memory makes him, again and again, rejoice.

At the gate of the Bhagavad-Gita there stands a line. It is a line that dares and discourages the translator who thinks of stepping across it:

dharmakshetre kurukshetre

Twin tetrasyllables in tight succession, a construction altogether untranslatable. Or at least untranslatable with either the grace of prose or the grace of verse.

"On the field of dharma, on the field of the Kurus" proliferates articles, making a mouthful out of Sanskrit's efficient yokewords. "On Dharma Field, on Kuru Field" makes it seem like "Dharma Field" is a place name, when it's really a metaphor for an actual place, Kurukshetra (which exists to this day), where dharma and adharma battle it out. The line is perfect because it sets the literal and figurative scene for the entire poem in a single line, the two halves of the line balanced as though by an equal sign.

I remain dissatisfied with my own solution—"On that field of dharma, Kurukshetra"—but I love how much I had to think about it. That probably explains why I decided to translate the *Gita* in the first place. I wanted a closer way to read it.

౭

Translate—to move something in space—and *metaphor*—to carry over—are related in their Greek and Latin etymologies. To make metaphor or to make a translation, you have to keep moving. You aim to move a reader by moving words about.

Ideally, in the flush of inspiration, the words move on

their own. Translation doesn't quite give you the sense of "automatic writing," of language coming alive and seizing free will for itself—at least not if you are finicky-faithful to your original text. It is hard work the whole way through.

Sanskrit's grammar, like Latin's, is flexible about word order. Sometimes I felt the word order was important to the meaning, and in those cases, I preserved it carefully. In other instances, I reserved the right to shift a clause from its place within the Sanskrit *sloka* to a new location in its corresponding English sentence. Sanskrit also has a tendency to construct sentences in the passive voice. If you plugged the Sanskrit into a translation engine, most sentences would come out in the "This was done by him to me" format. Sometimes the passive voice struck me as crucial to accuracy of meaning, and I preserved it; other times, it's just a quirk of the language.

I once made a version in prose, but the Gita is, unabashedly, a poem. The Gita-poet, in fact, was actually something of a show-off. When Arjuna is starstruck by the cosmic form of the divine, he stammers and bows down as he asks a question. Or, as our poet would have it:

sa-gadgadam bhitabhita pranamya

"Kneeling, he spoke / To Krishna in a terror-struck stutter." A master technician of the verse line, the Gita-poet makes the Sanskrit line itself stammer twice, doubling the sounds *gad* and *bhit* in quick succession. That is only one example of the sly verbal marvels he pulls off. He does it even in the midst of a standard epic catalogue, playing with the warrior Bhima's name, calling him not by his name but describing him, instead, as *bhimakarma,* "fearsome in action." Elsewhere in the first session, the Gita-poet sets up a parallel between Bhima's name and the name of the opposing army's highest leader, Bhishma—quite readily contradicting history (Bhima was not, in fact, his own army's leader) for the sake of a sound effect. The poet sometimes privileges the ludic element in a way not usually expected of a scripture, although the first lines of Genesis contain their share of double meanings and self-delighting word-music, too, like that lovely phrase *tohu wabohu.* The Gita-poet is also enamored of anaphora. I have used the structural and musical resources of American verse to preserve these rhetorical and poetic elements wherever the English language, or my own abilities, made it possible.

~

The Gita is the scripture of multiplicity, and its multiplicity extends to its form and structure. Considered as a dialogue, it's actually *two* dialogues, nested one inside the other.

In the "frame story," the advisor Sanjaya speaks with the blind King Dhritarashtra. What Sanjaya says, for the most part, is the dialogue between Krishna and Arjuna, a story-within-the-story. Krishna, in a few instances, quotes verbatim the claims of rival philosophers about the universe—speaker quoting speaker quoting speaker.

But that is not the only formal multiplicity. The Gita's quatrains are cast in one of two different meters, most frequently the *sloka,* much more rarely the *tristubh.* Sometimes the poem skips for a stretch into the rarer meter, then reverts; in these cases, most commentators are at a loss as to why the poet chose to switch things up. Mere variety for variety's sake isn't the explanation, given that several of the longest didactic passages are in *sloka* meter straight through.

The only clearly deliberate use of the rarer meter occurs in the long run of *tristubh* quatrains in Session 11, when Arjuna beholds Krishna's Universal Form. Arjuna, Sanjaya, and Krishna himself all use this meter for the duration of the theophany. This sets apart that moment in the poem: During recitations, the music of the incantation changes, abruptly and unmistakably. The use in Session 11 also reflects Krishna's "expansion" because the verse line itself expands in the rarer meter. The expansion is so striking that I flirted, for a while, with printing the whole run in CAPS LOCK. Instead I have opted to "expand" the verse line itself.

The original Sanskrit does not rhyme, although there are plenty of other sound effects and intricate rhetorical structures. In this translation, the characters speak in two ways, also. All the characters except Krishna (who delivers the bulk of the Gita) speak in nonmetrical, sometimes spikily alliterative, often enjambed quatrains. Krishna speaks in a much more measured, regular verse. This embodies, formally, the contrast between the despairing, uncertain Arjuna and the calm, didactic Krishna. Arjuna's rhythm is irregular turbulence; Krishna's rhythm is mostly serene, except when he gets cosmic and expansive—and when he gets irritated, as in his snarling references to hypocritical priests and nihilists. Usually, when he is teaching Arjuna, his meter stays fairly regular.

This rule changes only for the expansive meter of the *tristubh* quatrains. This rule also changes at the very end of the poem, when Arjuna and Sanjaya both—having heard the Gita in its entirety, their inner turbulence resolved—"fall in" and match Krishna's rhythm.

Essentially, I have created and imposed a pattern, not present in the original poem, that represents its dynamic. Simultaneously I have preserved, by orchestrating different sounds for the *sloka* and *tristubh* meters, the pattern that *is* present in the original.

I had three advantages when approaching this project. I already knew the script of Sanskrit, the Devanagari, because it is the same as modern-day Hindi's; I have been studying this poem, and Hinduism generally, off and on for more than a quarter century; and I have spent the same amount of time studying, and practicing, the art of poetry.

These advantages were counterbalanced, and then some, by the fact that I had to translate from a dead language. All the instincts, all the instant implicit understandings in the languages I grew up speaking, English and Gujarati—these were out of reach when it came to Sanskrit, and permanently so. My eyes glazing over as I gazed at declension tables, I longed for somewhere I might travel to immerse myself. Sanskrit was far away, not geographically but temporally. There were not even television shows and movies I could watch to pick up the rhythms and connotations of the language, as I did in my boyhood with Hindi.

I knew I had to compensate for this lack of living exposure. I did it the only way possible: I made up with diligent knowledge for what I lacked in instinctive know-how. Accordingly, I made every last word of this poem its own little research project.

What was its meaning in nineteenth-century dictionaries prepared by British scholars, and how did those definitions compare to those in modern-day Sanskrit-English dictionaries? What was its root word? What was its etymology? What were its relatives in other Indo-European languages I might be familiar with, like Latin, French, or Greek—and did it find its way, through any of these channels, into English? Where else was it used in the Gita, and did its connotation change based on its context there? How did other translators translate it? What were the etymologies of potential English candidates, and did they match up? Finally—given that some of the worst translations of the Gita have issued from excellent Sanskritists—was this an instance in which I should privilege my instincts in the living language over my research in the dead one?

That is how I worked through this poem, twice. I have actually translated this poem three times now: Once, years ago, I rendered the first sessions in a singable, alliteration-studded English equivalent of the two meters of the original:

> *Krishna, I have no wish to kill,*
> *Keen to kill though my kinsmen are.*

The form required me to lose too much information in the transfer. A second time, I translated the Gita into highly conversational American prose, in screenplay format, with the commentary embedded in the dialogue as stage directions. It was probably more "accessible" than this version, but it wasn't a poem. Finally, with a nudge from my editor at Knopf, Deborah Garrison, I have translated this poem of more than one meter as a poem of more than one meter.

The Gita's meter is always strict, but I dilate and contract my counts as necessary, keeping up a regularity of rhythm for Krishna, as I mentioned. The original is strange: Its line length can carry, in one case, the same amount of information as three English monosyllables; the very next line packs down a treatise's worth of metaphysics.

The thing is done, and the reader can judge if the third time has been the charm. I suspect I will circle back to the Gita in the future at some point and have a fourth go at this. I am still haunted by my failed first attempt, for example; I still think it would be a signal feat of translation to make this Godsong actually singable in English as it is in Sanskrit. Maybe in my next version, if not in my next life.

༄

Three men once ventured into the part of an Indian rainforest known for a bird of paradise never photographed or caged before. That part of the rainforest was so dense, the birds of paradise were invisible. Only their songs could be heard crisscrossing the midnight under the canopy.

One man was an ornithologist whose research centered

on avian communication. He wheeled out his equipment with him, and after recording a snippet, he would clap enormous headphones on his ears and play it back, over and over, scribbling in a notebook, trying to figure out what each combination of notes meant. If only he could develop a grammar, his reasoning went, he could persuade the bird of paradise into a cage.

The second fellow, a bird-watcher with a camera, laughed at these ornithological labors. He pointed out that the birds of paradise were not "communicating," they were *singing,* which was something entirely different. Over years of trying to photograph this bird of paradise, he had gotten very good at its call. So he puckered his lips and flared his nostrils and let out a run of heavenly coloratura. He sounded, to the ornithologist, exactly like a bird of paradise; but the birds of paradise knew the difference and broke out into a clamor that sounded a lot like laughter. That run of notes was fine-sounding nonsense. It was nothing an actual bird of paradise would actually sing or say or even think. It was just the imitation of a sound. Or rather, it was a human being reproducing what a human being thought a bird of paradise should sound like.

The third man was neither an ornithologist nor a veteran bird-watcher. He was nothing at all, in fact, except a poet in love with paradise, everything about it, including its birds. His advantage was that he hadn't *always* been a human being. In his past life, he had been a bird of paradise himself—so what fascinated his companions as something exotic fascinated *him* as something familiar. He strolled out and recited a poem about paradise in the human language he was used to, and the birds of paradise recognized their long-lost cousin right away.

That dense rainforest canopy came to life, opening black eyes and flaring green-gold crests. Leaf-green wings thrown wide, the birds of paradise flew off their perches. The canopy thinned, and sunlight poured down on ornithologist and bird-watcher and poet alike, but the birds of paradise settled on the shoulders and outstretched arms of the poet alone. The two others hurried forward, one with his open cage, one with his camera, but the poet told the birds to hurry and fly back up to their invisible perches. And that is what they did—only they took him with them, bearing him aloft with so many gently pinching birdfeet, to be their guest awhile. When he closed his eyes he felt like he was flying.

Amit Majmudar

Amit Majmudar lives in Ohio with his wife and three children.

A NOTE ON THE TYPE

This book was set in Granjon, a type named in compliment to Robert Granjon, a type cutter and printer active in Antwerp, Lyons, Rome, and Paris from 1523 to 1590. Granjon, the boldest and most original designer of his time, was one of the first to practice the trade of typefounder apart from that of printer.

COMPOSED BY NORTH MARKET STREET GRAPHICS, LANCASTER, PENNSYLVANIA

PRINTED AND BOUND BY BERRYVILLE GRAPHICS, BERRYVILLE, VIRGINIA

DESIGNED BY IRIS WEINSTEIN